INNER CITY POVERTY
IN PARIS AND LONDON

Reports of the Institute of Community Studies

A catalogue of the books available in the series **Reports of the Institute of Community Studies** and other series of social science books published by Routledge & Kegan Paul will be found at the end of this volume.

INNER CITY POVERTY
IN PARIS AND LONDON

Charles Madge and Peter Willmott

ROUTLEDGE AND KEGAN PAUL
LONDON, BOSTON AND HENLEY

First published in 1981
by Routledge & Kegan Paul Ltd
39 Store Street,
London WC1E 7DD,
9 Park Street,
Boston, Mass. 02108, USA and
Broadway House,
Newtown Road,
Oxon RG9 1EN
Printed in Great Britain by
Biddles Ltd
Guildford, Surrey

British Library Cataloguing in Publication Data

Madge, Charles
Inner city poverty in Paris and London.
1. Socially handicapped - London
2. Slums - London
3. Socially handicapped - Paris
4. Slums - Paris
I. Title   II. Willmott, Peter
303. 4'50941'421   HV4047.L/

ISBN 0-7100-0819-8

CONTENTS

ACKNOWLEDGMENTS   xi

INTRODUCTION   1

The broader context   3
The districts and the samples   3
Structure of the samples   5
Defining 'poverty'   8

I THE INNER CITY ENVIRONMENT   11

Past and present: Folie-Méricourt   11
Past and present: Stockwell   14
Environmental likes and dislikes   15
The social environment   19
Length of residence and the sense of community   20
The wish to leave the district   21
Environmental disadvantage, real and perceived   25

II HOUSEHOLD INCOMES: The national and
metropolitan context   27

Household incomes in Britain and France   28
How incomes changed in Britain and France, 1962-70   30
Occupation and income in London and Paris   33

III INCOME INEQUALITY AND POVERTY: Stockwell
and Folie-Méricourt   37

Unequal incomes   44
Poverty in Stockwell and Folie-Méricourt   46
Inner city poverty: an evaluation   52

IV   THE INNER CITY HOUSING PROBLEM   55

      Origins of the housing problem   55
      Overcrowding   58
      Lack of housing amenities   61
      Tenure: a changing pattern   64

V   EDUCATION, HEALTH AND LEISURE   73

      Educational disadvantage   73
      Health and disability   77
      Holidays and leisure activities   77

VI   MULTIPLE DISADVANTAGE   87

      Disadvantages in localities   87
      Multiple disadvantage: Stockwell and
           Folie-Méricourt   88
      Some disadvantaged families   90
      Who is multiply disadvantaged?   93
      Patterns of disadvantage   102

VII   COMPARISONS AND POLICIES   107

      Poverty and inequality   108
      Housing and environment   111
      Education, health and leisure   111
      Comparative perspective   113

      APPENDIX I   Additional tables   116

      APPENDIX II   Analyses of multiple disadvantage 122

      REFERENCES   129

      INDEX   132

TABLES

Intro.1   Occupational classification, Stockwell and
Folie-Méricourt   6

Intro.2   Occupations of heads of household: households
with two or more children, Stockwell and Folie-
Méricourt, 1973   7

Intro.3   National origin of heads of household: households with two or more children, Stockwell and
Folie-Méricourt, 1973   8

I.1   Environmental likes and dislikes in Stockwell,
England or Greater London, and Folie-Méricourt   16

I.2   Physical and social dislike of the environment:
households with two or more children, Stockwell
and Folie-Méricourt, 1973   18

I.3   The wish to move by occupation and national
origin of heads of household: households with
two or more children, Stockwell and Folie-
Méricourt, 1973   24

I.4   The wish to move and the number of persons per
room: households with two or more children,
Stockwell and Folie-Méricourt, 1973   24

II.1   Occupation of heads of household   28

II.2   Net income per household and per head by occupation of head of household: UK 1971, France 1970   30

II.3   Net weekly income at 1962 prices for three broad
occupational groups of households: UK and France,
1962 and 1970   31

II.4   Ratio of net incomes of 'self-employed, professional and managerial' households to those of
'other non-manual and manual' households: UK
and France, 1962 and 1970   32

II.5   Occupation of economically active males: UK,
Greater London, Inner London, 1971; France,
Paris agglomération, Paris, 1968   34

III.1   Number of children per household by national
origin of head of household: households with two
or more children, husbands earning, Stockwell
and Folie-Méricourt, 1973   46

III.2   Household weekly income net of housing costs per
equivalent adult, by occupation and national origin
of head of household: households with two or more
children, husbands earning, Stockwell and Folie-
Méricourt, 1973   47

III.3 Ratio between the income per equivalent adult of the highest and lowest occupational and national origin groups of household: households with two or more children, husbands earning, Stockwell and Folie-Méricourt, 1973 47

III.4 Proportion of households in 'poverty' and 'severe poverty', by occupation of head of household: households with two or more children, Stockwell and Folie-Méricourt, 1973 49

III.5 Proportion of households in 'poverty' and 'severe poverty' by national origin of head of household: households with two or more children, Stockwell and Folie-Méricourt, 1973 51

III.6 Proportion of households in 'poverty' and 'severe poverty', with and without an earning husband, by national origin of head of household: households with two or more children, Stockwell and Folie-Méricourt, 1973 52

IV.1 The age of the housing stock in England and France 55

IV.2 Overcrowding and severe overcrowding by occupation and national origin of head of household: households with two or more children, Stockwell and Folie-Méricourt, 1973 60

IV.3 Proportion of households with three basic housing amenities: UK and France, 1961 onwards 62

IV.4 Proportion with less than four and less than two basic housing amenities, by occupation and national origin of head of household: households with two or more children, Stockwell and Folie-Méricourt, 1973 65

IV.5 Proportion of households in three main housing tenures: UK and France, Inner London and Paris, Stockwell and Folie-Méricourt; households with two or more children, 1973 66

IV.6 Proportion of households in three housing tenures by occupation and national origin of head of household: households with two or more children, Stockwell and Folie-Méricourt, 1973 71

IV.7 Overcrowding and lack of housing amenities by housing tenure: households with two or more children, Stockwell and Folie-Méricourt, 1973 72

V.1 Age of head of household at completion of education, by occupation and national origin: households with two or more children, Stockwell and Folie-Méricourt, 1973 76

V.2 Limiting illness or disability of one or more members of the household, by occupation and national origin of head of household: households with two or more children, Stockwell and Folie-Méricourt, 1973 78

V.3 Proportion of households where no holiday taken in previous twelve months, by occupation and national origin of head of household: households with two or more children, Stockwell and Folie-Méricourt, 1973   80

V.4 Proportion of heads of household taking part in ten leisure activities in previous month: households with two or more children, Stockwell and Folie-Méricourt, 1973   81

V.5 Types of leisure activity and total number of activities in previous month reported by heads of household, by occupation and national origin: households with two or more children, Stockwell and Folie-Méricourt, 1973   82 & 83

V.6 Proportion of heads of household disadvantaged and severely disadvantaged in respect of leisure, by occupation and national origin: households with two or more children, Stockwell and Folie-Méricourt, 1973   85

V.7 Stockwell and Folie-Méricourt compared by types of disadvantage   86

VI.1 Proportion of households with five kinds of disadvantage and severe disadvantage: households with two or more children, Stockwell and Folie-Méricourt, 1973   89

VI.2 Proportion of households with different numbers of disadvantages and severe disadvantages: households with two or more children, Stockwell and Folie-Méricourt, 1973   90

VI.3 'Expected' compared with 'observed' proportions with different numbers of disadvantages and severe disadvantages: households with two or more children, Stockwell and Folie-Méricourt, 1973   95

VI.4 Average number of disadvantages and severe disadvantages, by occupation and national origin of head of household: households with two or more children, Stockwell and Folie-Méricourt, 1973   97

VI.5 Average number of disadvantages and severe disadvantages, by education, housing tenure, family status and number of children: households with two or more children, Stockwell and Folie-Méricourt, 1973   99

VI.6 The proportion with each of five disadvantages among households with three or more disadvantages compared with the proportion with these disadvantages among all households, households with two or more children, Stockwell and Folie-Méricourt, 1973   104

VI.7   Proportion of households with combinations of two,
       three and four out of five disadvantages: house-
       holds with two or more children, Stockwell and
       Folie-Méricourt, 1973   105
VII.1 Components of personal income as percentages
       of income: France, UK, 1960, 1970, 1974   113
VII.2 Direct and indirect taxes and social security
       contributions as percentages of income: France,
       UK, 1960, 1970, 1974   113
AI.1   Length of time in district by occupation and
       national origin of heads of household: house-
       holds with two or more children, Stockwell and
       Folie-Méricourt, 1973   116
AI.2   Sources of household income and direct tax paid,
       by occupation of head of household: UK 1971,
       France 1970   117
AI.3   Net income of households with different cate-
       gories of self-employed heads, France 1970   118
AI.4   Household income per week and its sources, by
       occupation of head of household: households
       with two or more children, husband earning,
       Stockwell and Folie-Méricourt, 1973   119
AI.5   Household income per week and its sources, by
       national origin of head of household: house-
       holds with two or more children, husband
       earning, Stockwell and Folie-Méricourt, 1973   120
AI.6   Proportion of wives working and contribution
       to household income per working wife, by
       occupation and national origin of head of
       household: households with two or more children,
       husbands earning, Stockwell and Folie-Méricourt,
       1973   121
AII.1 Contribution of household variables to house-
       holds' disadvantage scores   123
AII.2 Contribution of household variables to house-
       holds' severe disadvantage scores   124
AII.3 Factor analysis of disadvantages included in
       multiple disadvantage score   125
AII.4 Standardised scores of the seven household types
       in Stockwell   127
AII.5 Standardised scores of the seven household
       types in Folie-Méricourt   128

ACKNOWLEDGMENTS

This comparative study was supported by a grant from the
Social Science Research Council, which also helped earlier with
the arrangements for Willmott's Visiting Professorship in Paris
1972 and a subsequent short visit under the auspices of the
Centre National de la Recherche Scientifique. The study would
not have been possible without the encouragement of Clemens
Heller of the Maison des Sciences de l'Homme, Paris. The Institute of Community Studies and, later, the Centre for Environmental Studies provided essential support.

The study in Folie-Méricourt was carried out with great energy
by Pierre Aiach, who wrote the report on that work for the
French Government. Thanks are due to him and his colleagues
at the Division de la Recherche Médico-Sociale, Institut National
de la Santé et de la Recherche Médicale, and likewise to Graeme
Shankland and his colleagues of the Shankland Cox Partnership
who, in association with a team from the Institute of Community
Studies, carried out the Lambeth Inner Area Study under con-
tract for the Department of the Environment.

Wyn Tucker (of the Institute of Community Studies) helped in
countless ways, including work on the re-analysis of the Stockwell data. Rose Deakin also helped with that analysis, as did Ian
Cullen (of University College London), who was in particular
responsible for the multiple regression and the factor analysis.
Mark Shaw (of the Centre for Environmental Studies) prepared
the cluster analysis and drafted the relevant section of Appendix
2. Michael Young made helpful suggestions on the draft. Phyllis
Willmott gave invaluable advice, particularly on French and
British social policies, though we have sometimes differed from
her on interpretation.

The various drafts were typed by Pauline Bennington, Doris
Cook, Nicola Escott, Ann Mead, Francine Miller, Mary McManus
and, above all, Christine Marchant.

INTRODUCTION

Paris and London are majestic world cities, whose names can conjure up countless paired images: the Place de la Concorde and Trafalgar Square, the Rue de Rivoli and Regent Street, the Luxembourg Gardens and St James's Park, boulevard cafés and Victorian pubs, art-nouveau Métro stations and red-white-and-blue labelled Undergrounds, green single-decker buses and red double-deckers. Each city is a national magnet, a political, commercial and cultural giant. But each is at the same time home to millions of ordinary people, most of whom live not in Mayfair or the Faubourg Saint Honoré, Bloomsbury or the Quartier Latin, but in districts known only by name, if at all, even to their fellow Londoners or Parisians. Two such everyday metropolitan neighbourhoods are the subject of this book, which is to our knowledge the first Paris/London 'tale of two cities' ever recounted by social researchers.

Stockwell, in the London Borough of Lambeth, and Folie-Méricourt, in the 11th arrondissement of Paris, are alike in that both are 'inner areas' of their respective cities, their populations mainly 'working-class' but with a cosmopolitan mix of social and national origins. They differ in many ways, not least in that one is English (and London) and the other French (and Parisian). The combination of similarities and differences is the reason for this comparative study of poverty. If such cross-national comparisons are to be useful to policy, two conditions need to be met. The first is that the issues they face are recognisably alike. The second is that there is enough variation - in the circumstances and in the measures adopted by public authorities - to suggest some conclusions.

Although we believe that these criteria are satisfied, the two areas were not initially selected to be compared with each other. Folie-Méricourt was picked for study by Willmott in 1972, in collaboration with a French colleague, Pierre Aiach. The idea of local research into 'cumulative inequality' (to translate literally from the French) was conceived in the course of Willmott's three-month visiting professorship in Paris in that year. An application was made to the research arm of the French government's central planning office (Commissariat Général du Plan) for a study to be carried out by Aiach, working in the medico-social division of the national institute of health and medical research (INSERM). under Willmott's direction. The project started in 1973 and the report on it was written in 1975 (Aiach, 1975). Folie-Méricourt was chosen as a result of a process of statistical comparison of

1

quartiers of Paris, partly because it had a high proportion of
manual workers and immigrants, and partly because its housing
was as bad as anywhere in the city.

If the French area was chosen by the researchers, the British
one was at least partly chosen by the then Secretary of State
for the Environment, Peter Walker. The time was again 1972, and
the study began at the end of that year, with most of the interviewing being done, as in Folie-Méricourt, in 1973. The borough
of Lambeth was selected by Walker as a suitable inner area in
London, to be examined alongside similar areas in Liverpool and
Birmingham, and the Stockwell study area within Lambeth was
suggested by the research team on the basis of an examination
of data for the whole borough. Whereas Folie-Méricourt was an
administrative area (each arrondissement of Paris being divided
into four administrative 'quarters'), the Stockwell study area
was not. Because the various functional boundaries used by central and local government in Lambeth, as elsewhere in British
cities, did not correspond (see Shankland et al., 1977), it would
have been impossible to define a similar kind of administrative
area to that used in Paris. The study area was picked as containing the characteristic inner city problems and as having some
geographical coherence, being bounded by a railway line and
three major roads (for details of the selection procedure, see
Shankland Cox Partnership/Institute of Community Studies, 1974).

The Lambeth study as a whole, which ended in 1976, was
broader and more ambitious than the relatively small-scale enquiry in Paris, and the interest in poverty and disadvantage
figured as only part of the brief. Like the parallel studies in
Liverpool and Birmingham, it was intended to take a comprehensive look at inner city problems, combining research and action
projects in such a way as to 'provide a base for general conclusions on policies and action'. The work was carried out by a
joint team from the Shankland Cox Partnership and the Institute
of Community Studies. Willmott was, with Graeme Shankland,
co-director of the whole study, and had particular responsibility
for, amongst other things, the main household survey which provides the basis of the statistical data used in this book and the
study of multiple disadvantage (see Shankland Cox Partnership/
Institute of Community Studies, 1975b, 1975c and 1977a).

Thus the two studies were conceived and designed separately,
though it had been hoped from the outset that the Paris enquiry
might be matched by one in London. On Willmott's return from
Paris in the summer of 1972, he was asked by Shankland whether
he would like to participate in the Lambeth Inner Area Study,
and from then on a comparison was always a possibility. The project did not come alive until after the publication of the final report of the Lambeth Inner Area Study (Shankland et al., 1977),
when Madge and Willmott planned this study and applied to the
Social Science Research Council for some support with the research costs.

THE BROADER CONTEXT

The studies were of conditions of life of some families as they were in 1973. The districts have changed since then, as have the social policies of both countries, so in this sense the comparison is out of date. An important example is the change, in Britain, from family allowances to child benefits and the increase in their real value; this change narrowed, though by no means closed, the gap in family support in the two countries.

At an early stage we decided to set the local studies in the context of national and, where available, metropolitan data. We would use the information from the two local enquiries as case studies, illustrating and amplifying metropolitan and national differences; or, to put it the other way round, by looking at the broader setting, we would try to deepen understanding of what was happening locally. In the event, we believe that we have been able to make national and metropolitan comparisons that have not been drawn before. Comparative data on national and metropolitan bases are, however, uneven and in consequence the extent to which we have been able to use them varies from chapter to chapter.

We have drawn upon government survey material for national figures. In Britain, for instance, we used the reports of the Family Expenditure Surveys and the General Household Surveys; in France our main source was the various analyses reported in the government publication 'Économie et Statistique'. We were inevitably constrained by the exigencies of the material, and have therefore been obliged to make the best of what we could get. Usually, for example, our results are presented in terms of heads of households, but sometimes of economically active men. We have sometimes had to combine categories which we would have preferred to have kept separate. Sometimes, as we have said, no useful information was available at all. Despite the difficulties, we believe there is potential for future comparisons, a point we take up again in the final chapter.

For metropolitan comparisons, the area that best matches Greater London is the Paris agglomération including the city of Paris with its 20 arrondissements and extending beyond it to the three adjoining departments of the petite couronne (Hauts-de-Seine, Seine-St-Denis and Val-de-Marne). At the 1971 Census, 13 per cent of the British population lived in Greater London, and at the 1968 Census 13 per cent of the French population lived in the Paris agglomération. Paris itself in 1968 contained 2.6 million residents, while in 1971 inner London had nearly three million.

THE DISTRICTS AND THE SAMPLES

We have already said something about Stockwell and Folie-Méricourt, and they are described more fully in Chapter 1. The

main point about them is that they can in our view reasonably
be compared as representative of the inner areas of their
respective cities. No inner city area is 'typical' of the city of
which it is part, and Folie-Méricourt is probably less so of Paris
than Stockwell of Inner London. But the two places are similar
in their distance from the central area (bearing in mind the
greater density of Paris than London). They also shared
important characteristics: a high proportion of manual workers,
especially those with limited skills; a high proportion of immigrants; and, particularly in Folie-Méricourt, a legacy of substandard housing.

The most visible contrast between the two places, reflecting
what we have just said about density, is that Folie-Méricourt is
much more closely packed than Stockwell. There are broad
boulevards at its eastern and western boundaries, but in between is a dense grid of narrow streets and alleys, with hardly
a blade of grass or a tree. The buildings of the quartier vary
in their state of repair and the quality of their amenities, but
they are essentially much alike - the six and seven-storey
appartement blocks so characteristic of their city.

Stockwell too is bounded by broad main roads, though they
are not as tree-lined as Paris boulevards. It is also cut through
by other major roads which intersect at the road junction by the
underground station that bears its name. Even on these major
roads, and to a much greater extent behind them, Stockwell
presents a more diverse face than its Paris counterpart. There
are streets and crescents of well-preserved Georgian and early
Victorian houses, 'oases' as they were called in the report of the
Lambeth Inner Area Study. There are streets of tall Victorian
terraces in red brick. There are short roads of two-storey
terraced houses, usually in London stock brick. The greatest
variety has been introduced by the intervention of the local
councils - the Lambeth Council, the Greater London Council
and its predecessor, the London County Council. There are
four-storey neo-Georgian estates, patchworked with grass rect-
angles. There are post-war blocks of four-storey maisonettes, a
double-decker version of the traditional terrace. There are the
almost universally disliked tower blocks, rising above the rest
of the skyline. There are more recent low-rise high-density
estates, with landscaped children's playgrounds, 'pedestrian
walkways' and vandalised underground garages.

In using our survey data to study the two places we were,
as with national statistics, again constrained. In particular, the
sampling method was different. In Folie-Méricourt an early
decision was made to interview a small sample intensively, and
this choice limited the comparisons that would later be drawn
with Stockwell. If the intensive study in Folie-Méricourt were to
be useful, its sample had to be relatively homogeneous; and
families with children were selected as being of particular
interest in a study of cumulative inequality. In seeking access
to a sample of such people, the help had been sought of the

family allowance organisation for the city of Paris (the Caisse d'Allocations Familiales). This body was willing to help in drawing a sample, but its records were confined to certain categories of family: those with two or more children aged seventeen or under (the minimum school-leaving age) and with self-employed non-professional people and central government employees excluded (because both of these kinds of family receive their family allowance through other channels). The number of households which were interviewed and which satisfied these conditions was 119, though the Aiach report (1975) included in the analysis a further nineteen households where it was found, on interview, that the circumstances had changed and the criteria no longer applied.

Despite the fact that the Folie-Méricourt sample was limited to a relatively small proportion of the total population, it seemed to us that the sensible thing was to use matching data from Stockwell. We therefore selected, from the main Stockwell household survey sample covering all types of household, those which corresponded to the same criteria. The only difference, one that we have confirmed has made no appreciable difference to the comparisons, is that we thought it proper in Stockwell to use the British minimum school-leaving age (16) as the defining age limit for children. The number of eligible households in the Stockwell sample was 158 which, with re-weighting to allow for a deliberate bias in the initial main sample, became 216, the number which appears as the total in most of the Stockwell tables in this book. (The weighting procedure is explained in Shankland Cox Partnership/Institute of Community Studies, 1975a). Occasionally we draw upon data from the full re-weighted Stockwell samples of nearly 1200 households and, on opinion questions, of over 2000 adults.

STRUCTURE OF THE SAMPLES

It is obvious that the samples in the two areas on which we concentrate attention are not representative of the populations at large in the districts. Households composed of old people are excluded, as are households without children or with only one child, and likewise those whose head was self-employed or state-employed. Within the limits of the samples - relatively alike in their stage of life - we have split households up in various ways for the purposes of analysis. We needed, in essence, to do two things: to make sure that we compared like with like and to see how different dimensions of poverty or inequality were distributed among the different types of household. As a background to the results presented later, we have to say something about the main divisions we made within the samples and about how the two places compared in terms of them.

One point should be cleared up at the beginning. We commonly use the term 'head of household', for example in talking about occupational status, national origin or education. The term, and the concept behind it, are being increasingly questioned by those who argue that to talk about 'heads' of households implies an acceptance - or worse, a reinforcement - of what is now an out-dated form of domestic arrangement.

We recognised the difficulty. But we felt bound to continue the familiar usage, for three reasons. The first was that we needed to see how our samples compared with national and metropolitan populations or samples and, in order to make such comparisons, were obliged to follow the conventions used in official statistics. The second was that they had in any case been adopted in both the original surveys in 1973. The third was that there seemed in practice to have been little uncertainty in our surveys about who the 'head' was. The definitions had turned on responsibility for housing, on who was the legal owner or tenant; if such responsibility was shared by a couple, the interviewers had, for the sake of tidiness, been told to treat the man as the 'head'. Thus when we talk about household heads, we refer to the man if there was a couple (whether married or not) and the lone parent, in practice usually the mother, in one-parent families.

One distinction to be made within each sample was in terms of occupational status. We took the main systems of occupational classification used in each country - Socio-economic Groups (SEGs) in Britain and Catégories socio-professionnelles (CSPs) in France - and combined them into a simplified four-fold scheme, as shown in Table Intro.1.

Table Intro.1   Occupational classification, Stockwell and Folie-Méricourt

Titles used in this report	Socio-economic Groups (Britain)	Catégories Socio-professionnelles (France)	Examples in Stockwell and Folie-Méricourt
Professional and managerial	Professional workers, employers and managers, intermediate non-manual workers	Cadres supérieurs, cadres moyens, professions libérales, patrons, petits commerçants, artisans	Marketing director, proprietor of small grocer's shop, schoolteacher
Other non-manual	Junior non-manual workers	Employés de bureau et de commerce	Clerk, school caretaker, shop assistant
Skilled manual	Skilled manual workers, foremen and supervisors (manual)	Ouvriers qualifiés, contremaîtres	Compositor, electrician, factory foreman
Semi-skilled and unskilled manual	Semi-skilled and unskilled manual workers, personal service workers	Ouvriers specialisés, manoeuvres, personnel de service	Assembly worker, building labourer, waiter/waitress

Sources: Office of Population Censuses and Surveys, 1971; Institut National de la Statistique et des Études Économiques, 1977

Heads of household in each district were classified according to this scheme. The resulting occupational structures are given in Table Intro.2. The last two categories shown in Stockwell did not occur in the Folie-Méricourt sample. The 'unoccupied' consisted of households whose head was neither employed nor seeking employment, but did not include those where the head was unemployed or off sick; they were either lone mothers or students. We discuss later the reasons why lone mothers were unoccupied in Stockwell but not in Folie-Méricourt. The 'inadequate information' category consisted of those households where the occupation of the head was not known; these appeared in Stockwell rather than Folie-Méricourt because the sample survey had been much larger, and less effort had been made than in Folie-Méricourt to check back on information not given in the initial interview.

Table Intro.2 *Occupations of heads of household: households with two or more children, Stockwell and Folie-Méricourt, 1973*

	Stockwell %	Folie-Méricourt %
Professional and managerial	9	18
Other non-manual	7	14
Skilled manual	33	34
Semi- or unskilled manual	32	34
Unoccupied	13	−
Inadequate information	6	−
Total	100	100
Number	216	119

We show later that the proportion of 'professional and managerial' heads of households was lower in both samples than in London or Paris as a whole, and the proportion with manual worker heads was correspondingly high. As Table Intro.2 shows, in Folie-Méricourt and Stockwell alike, the manual workers were evenly divided between those who had skill qualifications, on the one hand, and those who were semi-skilled or unskilled, on the other.

Another major dimension for analysis is national origin. This, rather than nationality or ethnicity, separates households with immigrant heads from those with heads born in Britain or France. Thus when we use the term 'British', it should be taken to mean born in Britain rather than having British nationality. Table Intro.3 shows that, in both samples, households with immigrant heads and those with heads born in Britain or France were almost equally divided. In each area a particular group of immigrants - the North Africans in Folie-Méricourt and even more the

West Indians in Stockwell - were especially conspicuous. But other immigrants were also numerous. In Stockwell they included households from Nigeria, Spain, Eire, Cyprus, India, Portugal and Mauritius, and in Folie-Méricourt from Spain, Portugal, the West Indies, Yugoslavia and Italy.

Table Intro.3   National origin of heads of household: households with two or more children, Stockwell and Folie-Méricourt, 1973

Stockwell	%	Folie-Méricourt	%
West Indian	30	North African	16
Other non-British	25	Other non-French	33
British	45	French	51
Total	100		100
Number	216		119

The influence of national origin on occupation was more evident in Folie-Méricourt than Stockwell. In Stockwell, for example, semi-skilled and unskilled heads made up 35 per cent among West Indians, 36 per cent among other immigrants, and 27 per cent among British-born. In Folie-Méricourt, semi-skilled or unskilled accounted for 74 per cent of North Africans, 38 per cent of other non-French and 20 per cent of French-born. There were no 'professional and managerial' heads among North Africans, 8 per cent among other non-French, but 30 per cent among French-born.

Family composition also varied with national origin. For example, the proportion of one-parent families, which was higher in Stockwell than in Folie-Méricourt, was particularly high among the Stockwell West Indians - a quarter against about one in ten among other households. In Folie-Méricourt, the percentage of one-parent households was the same in the different national origin groups. In both districts about half the households contained just two children; West Indians and North Africans were alike in having larger families than others, but whereas the proportion with four or more children was about a third among West Indians, it was well over half among North Africans.

DEFINING 'POVERTY'

Our central purpose was to see how households compared between and within the districts in terms of poverty, including its multiple forms. But what general term were we to use for dimensions of 'poverty' other than income?

One possibility was 'deprivation', a word that we have our-

selves used in the context of this kind of discussion in the past.
It can be argued that, though 'deprivation' literally means having had something taken away, it can legitimately be used more
broadly because, as it was put in a Lambeth Inner Area Study
report on 'multiple deprivation', 'in ordinary usage it has come
to mean not having something that a person might reasonably
expect to have' (Shankland Cox Partnership/Institute of Community Studies, 1977a). But we ourselves no longer find this
argument convincing. The more that we have read and reflected
on the matter, the more we have become persuaded by the argument of Rutter and Madge (1976, pp. 1-2) that 'deprivation' is
so vague a term and is employed in so many diverse senses that
it is no longer useful.

Rutter and Madge favoured the expression, 'disadvantage'.
Since it is as imprecise and as much of a portmanteau as
'deprivation', the alternative is perhaps not much of an improvement. In our view, however, it is to be preferred because it
does not contain the misleading, and sometimes emotively used,
suggestion that something has been taken away. We propose,
therefore, to use the term 'disadvantage' to refer to the main
subject of this book.

How then are the various disadvantages to be defined? This
is a question that arises with most chapters and particularly
with Chapter VI, where we consider the extent to which disadvantages are found together in the same family.

From time to time we use data from one district only, without
being able to make a comparison with the other, but for the most
part we concentrate on those disadvantages for which the surveys in the two districts provided adequate information on a
sufficiently comparable basis. There were five of these: low
income, overcrowding, lack of housing amenities, poor health
and limited leisure.

A familiar problem with analyses of the kind we proposed to
make is defining such disadvantages. We had, on each of the
five dimensions, to choose appropriate 'cut-off' points - the
levels below which a household would be judged as 'disadvantaged'. Should we adopt the same cut-off points in both
districts or instead take account of the different standards that
applied in each? With housing, for example, should we use a
British measure of overcrowding for Stockwell and a French for
Folie-Méricourt, or should we use the same measure for both?
We decided to use the same set of definitions in both places. We
saw no reason to believe that families in Folie-Méricourt wanted
or in any meaningful sense 'needed' less space, for instance, or
fewer amenities than families in Stockwell. We introduce these
various measures in the process of discussing different aspects
of disadvantage in the districts from Chapter III onwards; then
we summarise the definitions and bring them together in Chapter
VI.

In presenting our data, we follow the usual statistical rule and
in general draw attention to differences only if the probability

is less than one in 20 that they would have arisen by chance. When we give names, in quoting people's remarks or using their circumstances for the purpose of illustration, those names are fictitious to preserve confidentiality.

We had to decide what to do about changes in prices and incomes over the period since the two studies were done: we realised that the original figures would mean little to the reader. We decided against simply up-dating to mid-1980, when the book went to press, for two reasons. First, the research had, after all, been carried out at a particular point in time, and there seemed some advantage in retaining the historical context. Second, such a revaluation would not in itself have solved the problem, since those who came to the book in later years would be similarly nonplussed. We decided to revalue incomes and prices to mid-1980 levels, using changes in the British retail price index, and to include the new figure alongside that for the earlier year. For example, we show that in 1973 one Stockwell woman was earning £21 (mid-1980 prices: £59.64) and one Folie-Méricourt man the equivalent of £39.32 (1980: £111.67). We believe there is some value in having two such benchmarks instead of one.

We have already given some indication about the structure of the rest of the book. Chapter I presents, by way of background, something about the two districts as environments, showing how they have developed within their respective cities; it also considers how these environments are perceived by the people living in them. Chapters II to V look in turn at more objectively measurable kinds of disadvantage, in income, housing, education, health and leisure. Chapter VI examines the extent to which these disadvantages go together. Chapter VII tries to summarise and to draw some conclusions both for future research and for policy.

I

THE INNER CITY ENVIRONMENT

The inner areas of large cities are a mosaic of differing environments, some favourable and some adverse. Moreover, families and individuals differ in their response to the same environment, some finding it congenial, others wanting to escape from it as soon as possible. In this chapter we are not concerned with the environment inside the home, but with its ambience of streets, shops and open spaces, and, looking at it from the point of view of an individual person or household, with the social environment created by the people living around. Because the concept of environmental disadvantage combines an objective with a highly subjective component, it is less easy to measure than disadvantages like poverty or overcrowding, but it is important none the less - so much so, in our view, that we start with it, setting the scene by describing the two districts and by assessing the response to them of the people in our samples.

Stockwell and Folie-Méricourt both now lie close to the centre of their cities, but at the end of the eighteenth century each was on the rural fringe of a growing metropolis. Over about two centuries there was first a vast increase in the populations of Paris and London, and then a decline as people moved out to the suburbs and beyond. The trends were similar but the timing different. Inner London's population peak was around the time of the 1911 Census: the Paris peak was forty years later. Inner Paris is still one of the most densely populated cities in the world; inner London has reached a stage where the worry is that population may already have fallen too much for economic survival. We look now in turn at each study area and how it developed into the environment it was at the time of the surveys.

PAST AND PRESENT: FOLIE-MÉRICOURT

In Folie-Méricourt manufacturing industry appeared on a small scale early in the nineteenth century. The number of factories and workshops grew, until by 1880 the 11th arrondissement had one of the highest densities of population in Paris. It has continued to claim this distinction; the rate of building has never caught up with the growth of the population.

The Haussmann reconstruction of Paris (1850-70) drove wide avenues through the area and created large new squares, such as the Place de la République. Land made available under the Haussmann plan gave developers the opportunity to build new

middle-class dwellings along the avenues, as well as drab tenements for workers, the boîtes à loyer, towards which the state
gave a subsidy. But many of the workers, who had to live near
their jobs, were driven inwards into the blocks behind the tall
houses of the avenues which deprived them of air and sunlight
(Szulc, 1966; Maréchal and Tallard, 1973).

Dwellings, workshops, small businesses and storage depots
were intermeshed building by building, on different floors of
the same building or even between different rooms on the same
floor. Sites for industrial use crept in everywhere, reducing the
size of the inner courtyards, which under new regulations were
allowed a minimum area of seven square metres in place of the
previous twenty-five square metres, while the height limit of
five storeys was extended to seven storeys plus attics.

In 1893, a health register (casier sanitaire) of Paris housing
was created: a building where more than ten people died of
tuberculosis in a single year was declared insanitary and marked
down for early demolition. Results for the 11th arrondissement
in 1918 showed seventeen unhealthy blocks (ilôts) housing
200,000 people. By 1953 only one of these seventeen blocks had
been demolished. Part of the arrondissement was then declared
a redevelopment zone, and the prospect of demolition deterred
landlords from maintaining their buildings. In 1960, however, it
was officially admitted that no buildings were going to be des-
troyed: there would be no comprehensive redevelopment programme. After 1960 an increasing number of individual building
permits were granted even in zones previously declared unhealthy or due for comprehensive redevelopment.

Between the Censuses of 1954 and 1968, there were far-
reaching changes in the social composition of inner Paris,
particularly to the east and north. In 1954 there were, in terms
of the occupations of residents, twenty-three 'working-class'
quartiers in the eleven easterly arrondissements; by 1968 their
number had fallen to seven. In 1954, three of the four quartiers
in the 11th arrondissement had been 'working-class'; by 1968
there was only one, that being Folie-Méricourt.

The 1968 Census showed the contrasting social composition
on the two sides of the Avenue Parmentier, which divides the
quartier of Folie-Méricourt into an eastern, more working-class,
half and a western, more middle-class, one. The most working-
class blocks of all were at the eastern end of the eastern sector,
where in some the proportion of working-class households was as
high as 70 per cent. The immigrant population, more numerous
in Folie-Méricourt than in the rest of the arrondissement, increased by more than 20 per cent between 1962 and 1968.

From 1954 to 1968 there was much less new building in Folie-
Méricourt than elsewhere in the arrondissement, and what there
was included no social housing (HLM - habitations à loyer modéré)
compared with the 600 HLM dwellings built in the rest of the
arrondissement over the same period. From about 1968, the pace
of demolition and new construction quickened. At first the new

building was all in the more fashionable western sector, but the
developers increasingly turned their attention to the eastern
end. Their new interest in the 11th arrondissement was reflected
in land values. From 1970 to 1973 the price per square metre
almost doubled.

The contrasts within Folie-Méricourt were still sharp at the
time of the study. The character changed visibly as one walked
through the quartier from the Place de la République, at the
north-western corner, to the Boulevard de Belleville, its
eastern boundary. The Place de la République, part of the Paris
of the guidebooks, is a large green space, bounded and crossed
by busy roads and dominated by the central column 'to the
Republic', with bas-reliefs depicting historical episodes up to
1880. The seven major roads leading off the place include two
which serve as the northern and western boundaries of the
quartier and two more, Avenue de la République and Boulevard
Voltaire, which lead into it. These last two are lined with the
comfortable apartment blocks dating from Haussmann, and there
are similar, if slightly less grand, blocks in the nearby streets.

In 1974, the visitor who walked towards the heart of the
quartier saw how redevelopment was replacing some of the older
housing. In one street lists of demolition permits were posted. In
another, bulldozers were at work; further along the same street
cement mixers churned away and giant yellow cranes lowered
concrete foundations into place. In a third street the construction was further advanced: tall hoardings, illuminated by spot-
lights at night, announced that studios and apartments would
shortly be available for letting, with solarium, swimming pool,
interior gardens and underground parking; potential purchasers
were invited to enquire how they could 'live ten years ahead of
the times'.

Further still to the east the housing became noticeably more
derelict and cramped, in the narrow streets themselves and in
tiny courtyards and alleyways. In one court, ricketty brass
taps had notices above them declaring that the water was dangerous to drink. Inside the building a printed paper pinned on
the wall by the entrance announced that electricity improvements
were to be done soon. The push-button light on the stairs did
not work and one could see only a distant skylight at the top;
it was impossible to determine the colour of the crumbling
plaster on the walls. The wooden stairways were worn down and,
in places, broken away.

Towards the Boulevard de Belleville, Algerian and Tunisian
faces became more common. Arabs and Jews among them lived
side by side, without apparent hostility, and they retained
their distinctive cultures, their own cafés and their own shops.
One respondent in the sample, from Tunisia, was a 'ritual
supervisor' in a kosher slaughterhouse. An immigrant from
Algeria owned a café patronised almost exclusively by his Arab
compatriots. Near to each other in one street were a shop
specialising in couscous cooking pans, a grocery displaying

Algerian wine, a kosher butcher, a shop selling brightly
coloured Arab sweetmeats; the mingled smells were of oriental
spices and of cooking fritters.

The Boulevard de Belleville itself, just a kilometre from the
Place de la République, was lined with Arab and Jewish shops
and restaurants. Twice weekly a large open market filled the
central strip between its two carriageways. The low prices
attracted crowds of customers, including many French-born, and
the atmosphere was then even more cosmopolitan and lively than
at other times.

PAST AND PRESENT: STOCKWELL

In the first half of the nineteenth century, when Stockwell was
still a small village on the edge of London, several parts were
laid out as colonies for well-to-do refugees from the city. Small
groups of houses were arranged around a central feature - a
circus at Lansdowne Gardens, a crescent at Stockwell Park, a
small park at Durand Gardens. The buildings had imposing
entrances and large gardens, and were often of richly decor-
ated architecture: they were 'houses of character' and, after a
period of decline, many were subsequently restored to their
former glory. These were the 'oases' mentioned in the Introduction.

The rest of the area was rapidly built up at much higher
densities between 1850 and the outbreak of the First World War,
by which time a continuous sea of development joined Stockwell
to Brixton, Clapham, Kennington and Camberwell. Except for the
occasional small factory, shop or public building, most of this
was housing, for even then the typical resident travelled into
London to work. The houses were usually poorer cousins of the
buildings in the 'oases'; typically a three-storey Victorian terrace with bay windows and small front gardens.

The role of developer increasingly passed to the local authority. By 1976 there were seventeen major public housing estates,
nearly half of all households were council tenants and some two-
thirds of the land was in public ownership. Housing covered
over three-quarters of the area. The next biggest land use was
education, with four secondary schools and eleven primary.
There was little open space, the only sizeable park being at
Larkhall, a brave creation by the council over the previous ten
years. There were few factories, and shopping in the study
area was confined to a few minor parades and corner shops.

The area of Stockwell is four times larger than that of Folie-
Méricourt. Its population in 1973 was one fifth larger - in round
figures 50,000 compared with 40,000. So people in the Paris
quartier were living at more than three times the density of
their London counterparts. Much more sky was visible not only
in the main roads of Stockwell, but in the side roads and council
estates as well. Partly because of the council estates, housing

standards were in general far higher, in terms both of space
and amenities, in Stockwell than in Folie-Méricourt, as we show
in Chapter IV.

A perambulation through the area took longer than in Folie-
Méricourt because of the greater size. One similarity between
the two places was apparent if one approached Stockwell from
Brixton underground station, a few hundred yards outside the
study area. In and around Electric Avenue at Brixton was a
market as exotic as that in the central strip of the Boulevard de
Belleville near the Métro station of the same name. In Brixton,
as in the Paris street market, the crowds were of mixed ethnic
origin, but here with a Caribbean rather than a North African
flavour. As the visitor walked north-westwards from the south-
eastern corner of the Stockwell study area, there was again a
general impression of physical and social change, though with
much more of a mosaic pattern even than in Folie-Méricourt.
West Indians, for instance, were relatively concentrated in the
network of Victorian terraces around Landor Road, but they and
other immigrants also lived elsewhere in the study area, including the council estates.

The physical pattern was a complex one: the 'oases'; council
estates of all periods and styles; two- and three-storey
Victorian terraces. Some of the older housing was reasonably
well maintained, but much of it was not, and the most derelict
areas were small pockets of such older housing, usually multi-
occupied, together with some of the older local authority estates
- a reminder that, although council housing may have helped to
solve some problems, it is not without its own difficulties.

ENVIRONMENTAL LIKES AND DISLIKES

What did the residents themselves have to say about their districts? In both studies, they were asked a series of questions
about what they liked and disliked. In Stockwell, most of the
questions had wording identical with that used in an earlier
survey covering the whole of England. (This was carried out in
1972 by Social and Community Planning Research for the Department of the Environment. No report has been published, but the
Lambeth Inner Area Study Team had access to some of the findings.) So as to be able to compare Stockwell data with those in
the DOE survey, in Table I.1 we drew upon the full Stockwell
sample of 2035 adults interviewed in 1973 rather than the reduced sample of households with two or more children that we
use elsewhere. Similar, but not identical, questions were put to
the Folie-Méricourt sample of households with two or more children, though corresponding results are lacking for the rest of
the adult population, and for France and the Paris agglomération
as a whole.

In Folie-Méricourt most people had something good to say
about the quartier, whatever the final verdict. But the balance

was hostile. This is not surprising, since so much of the housing was in bad condition and there were few trees and little
grass. In Stockwell, too, the dominant impression from the
interviews was of relative discontent and of concern about current trends. Asked what they liked about the place, almost a
third of the full sample said 'nothing', whereas the comparable
proportion in England as a whole was no more than a seventh.
Asked whether they found their area 'attractive' or 'unattractive' to look at, over half of those who answered in Stockwell - but again about one in seven nationally - thought it unattractive. Nearly half the Stockwell people, in answer to a
question about whether they thought their district was 'improving or getting worse as a place to live in', said 'getting worse';
the proportion nationally was about a quarter.

*Table I.1   Environmental likes and dislikes in Stockwell, England or Greater
London, and Folie-Méricourt*

Likes	Stockwell [a] %	England [a] %	Folie-Méricourt [b] %
None	30	14	14
Good shopping facilities	18	22	30
Transport and access	39	29	27
Convenience for work	10	11	27
Schools	3	6	24
Nice people	11	25	8

Dislikes	Stockwell [a] %	Greater London [a] %	Folie-Méricourt [b] %
None	35	34	43
Immigrants, other people	21	17	40
Dirt, litter	13	2	29
Lack of facilities	7	9	32
Vandalism, crime	11	5	27
Lack of open space	3	–	37
Children, young people	8	5	–
Council services	7	9	–
Traffic	6	22	–
Other noise	6	6	32
Total number	2035	–	119

(a) General samples of adults.
(b) Parents with two or more children.
Total percentages of likes and dislikes add up to more than 100 per cent because some people
gave more than one answer.

The discontent was reflected in people's desire to move, a

matter dealt with more fully later. Though some who wanted to
move said they would prefer to remain in inner London, most
potential movers sought the semi-detached houses and green
spaces of suburbia, which they contrasted in their own minds
with the overcrowding, the unloved high-rise flats, the dirt and
litter, the resented newcomers, the crime and vandalism of the
inner city.

But this is only part of the story. After all, half the adults
in the Stockwell sample did not think the area was in decline.
Nearly a quarter actually thought it was improving. Over two-
thirds said they 'liked' some aspect of the district, usually its
accessibility to central London, to local shopping centres such
as Brixton, or to their work. At least as many adults wanted to
stay in the district as wanted to leave it.

Table I.1 shows that in Stockwell there were twice as many
who could think of nothing they 'liked' as in Folie-Méricourt or
in England as a whole. The proportions who had no 'dislikes'
were similar in Stockwell and Greater London, and not very
different in Folie-Méricourt.

Specific likes and dislikes generally bear on either the physical or social environment, though the two sometimes combine
or are coloured by each other. In Table I.2, the percentage
expressing physical and social dislike is related to the occupational group and national origin of heads of household, this
time only for households with two or more children.

The proportions registering physical and social dislike were
not dissimilar in the two places, though in Folie-Méricourt the
physical environment was disliked more often than the social.
The effect of national origin is seen in the relatively low figures
for dislike of both physical and social environments by the West
Indians compared to the British-born, but for social dislike
alone among immigrants as against the French-born in Folie-
Méricourt. The 'social' dislikes included complaints about 'immigrants', 'foreigners' or 'coloureds'; about vandalism or crime;
and about the behaviour of children or adolescents. Since at
least some of these complaints referred directly or indirectly to
immigrants, it is hardly surprising that in both Stockwell and
Folie-Méricourt immigrants were generally less critical of the
social environment. The lower level of physical dislike among
the Stockwell West Indians - not paralleled among the Folie-
Méricourt North Africans - suggests that they were also readier
than others to tolerate the physical aspects of the environment.

It is not always easy to separate complaints about housing
conditions from dislike of the wider physical environment, and
one can probably assume that in most people's minds they rein-
force each other. The most frequent criticism of the physical
environment outside the home was of dirt and litter, mentioned
by 13 per cent in the full Stockwell sample, compared to only 2
per cent in England as a whole. If we add complaints about
street cleaning and refuse disposal, the proportion complaining
in Stockwell was as high as one adult in six.

Table I.2   Physical and social dislike of the environment: households with two or more children, Stockwell and Folie-Méricourt, 1973

	Percentage in group expressing:							
	Physical dislike				Social dislike			
	Stockwell		Folie-Méricourt		Stockwell		Folie-Méricourt	
	%	Number in group	%	Number in group	%	Number in group	%	Number in group
Occupation of head of household								
Professional and managerial	53	19	67	21	58	19	57	21
Other non-manual	47	15	35	17	33	15	29	17
Skilled manual	51	71	40	40	37	71	23	40
Semi- and unskilled manual	34	68	56	41	41	68	37	41
Unoccupied	34	29	–	–	28	29	–	–
Inadequate information	36	14	–	–	50	14	–	–
National origin of head of household								
West Indian/ North African	34	65	58	19	25	65	32	19
Other non-British/ other non-French	47	53	44	39	34	53	18	39
British/French	50	98	52	61	51	98	49	61
All households	44	216	50	119	39	216	36	119

In Folie-Méricourt, the proportion complaining of dirt and litter was higher still. Complaints about noise other than traffic also figured largely, the noise often being identified as that made by other people, especially by North Africans and especially at night – an example of the difficulty of separating physical from social criticism. Complaints about the noise made by children were balanced by complaints about neighbours who would not tolerate children playing in the street, the only place where they could go. In Folie-Méricourt, two major sources of complaint were 'lack of facilities' and 'lack of open space', viewed primarily by the sample of families as a restriction of their children's activity and safety.

THE SOCIAL ENVIRONMENT

Many residents in both areas, as already indicated, said they
disliked the presence of particular kinds of people whom they
saw as different from themselves. About one in ten in the full
Stockwell sample complained in terms of other people's skin
colour or nationality. A similar proportion laid stress on what
they saw as 'rough', low-status or 'problem' families. Another
tenth or so complained about local children or teenagers.
Criticisms of young people were often linked to complaints about
vandalism and crime - again referred to by about one person in
ten:

> 'We dislike everything about the area. We keep ourselves
> to ourselves - there's no-one to really trust round here.
> It's no life for children here - they have to play indoors.
> There's break-ins when you go out. They tied an old
> woman up in her flat and robbed her. You can't trust a
> two-year-old here.'

There is no doubt that immigrants are a conspicuous feature
of the social environment in Stockwell and Folie-Méricourt alike.
As we pointed out in the Introduction, about half the heads of
household in both samples had been born abroad. Although
there were also large numbers of immigrants from other countries in Asia, Africa and Europe, West Indians tended to domin-
ate the perception by Stockwell residents of their social
environment, and it was the same with the North Africans in
Folie-Méricourt. In Stockwell, hostile attitudes and acts were
reported, both about blacks and whites and vice versa. Thus
Mrs Fletcher, a South Londoner by birth:

> 'The coloureds are arrogant trouble makers. They call
> you horrible names. You are over-swarmed with them.
> I'm the longest tenant on the estate and I've watched it
> deteriorate since coloured people arrived say five or six
> years ago. Coloured children spit on my children and
> call them "white trash". I've tried to be friendly with
> them but with little success. They have chips on their
> shoulders. I resent having "Black Power" written on the
> walls of the block.'

Mr Ngao, a Nigerian plumber: 'My child was bitten by a white
child and my wife had a bucket of water thrown at her head. My
girl had her glasses broken twice.'
  In Folie-Méricourt, people were asked specifically what they
thought about the residents of the quartier. Of all the responses,
a quarter were neutral, a quarter of the 'don't know' variety, a
quarter unfavourable and the remaining quarter broadly favourable. Only five replies were critical of racial intolerance, but the
interviewers noted that many of the foreign and North African

families seemed inhibited in replying on such matters. In people's comments, the quartier's dirtiness and lack of hygiene were sometimes linked to the presence of a foreign population.

LENGTH OF RESIDENCE AND THE SENSE OF COMMUNITY

As many as half of all households in the full Stockwell sample had been in their present home for less than five years, compared with about a third in Greater London and in Britain generally. Stockwell also had a high proportion of households who had moved three or more times in the five preceding years - 12 per cent as against 5 per cent in Britain as a whole. Compared with the full sample, however, households with two or more children were relatively settled in Stockwell. Of such households, the proportion who had lived in the district for less than five years was no more than just over a quarter. The proportion in the Folie-Méricourt sample was similar.

Length of time in the district has the advantage of being an objective measure. Presumably it has a bearing on such subjective matters as the development of a sense of community. Table AI.1 in Appendix I (p.116) compares the length of residence in the two study areas by occupation and national origin of heads of households. While the proportion of households in the samples with children who had lived in the district for less than five years was similar in the two districts, the proportion who had lived there for twenty or more years was larger in Stockwell than in Folie-Méricourt. Few of these established residents were immigrants - two in the Stockwell sample and two in Folie-Méricourt.

The relative instability of the Stockwell population would suggest that only a minority of people had relatives living nearby. Just under a third of adults turned out to have at least one within ten minutes' walk. Rather more people, about half, said they had at least one friend as near as this. People were asked about their contacts with these relatives or friends, and their answers were compared with a survey by the Institute of Community Studies in the London Metropolitan Region in 1970 (Young and Willmott, 1973). The comparisons suggested that contact with both friends and relatives was less common in Stockwell than elsewhere in the London Region. A direct comparison could not be made with the Institute's earlier study in Bethnal Green (Young and Willmott, 1957), but there seemed little doubt that kinship and community ties were weaker in the Stockwell of 1973 than in the East End of 1955.

One might also suppose that the presence of a relatively large proportion of newcomers might affect people's sense of locality. In Stockwell they were asked: 'Do you think there is an area round here that might be called your local neighbourhood - I mean the local area you live in or feel you belong to?' Only about a third of the full sample could recognise their local

'neighbourhood' in this way. In other places where the question
had been put, the proportion ranged from three-quarters to
nearly a hundred per cent (Shankland Cox and Associates, 1968;
Wilson and Womersley, 1969; Royal Commission on Local Government in England, 1969; Young, 1970).

The sense of locality varied in Stockwell according to people's
length of residence in the district: only one in six had it among
those who had been there for less than six months, as against
nearly half – still on the low side – among those who had lived
there for 20 or more years or who had been born there. The
high residential mobility of the population seems therefore to
have been one reason for the low sense of locality.

This 'neighbourhood' sense was not explored in Folie-Méricourt,
but questions were asked about contacts with parents, friends
and neighbours. About a third of those parents who were living
were seen once a week or more by heads of households, the proportion being much lower among the semi-skilled and unskilled,
and particularly those immigrants whose parents were living in
their country of origin. With these excluded, the proportion was
still low in comparison with even suburban areas in Britain
(Willmott and Young, 1960). Contacts with friends and neighbours also seemed in general rather low. Though most people
had some friends, few had much to do with other residents of
the quartier.

The data for both places are less full than we should like and
interpretation is correspondingly difficult, but we can at least
generalise that recent rapid physical and social change in both
districts had reduced the overall sense of community, though
paradoxically new communities had grown up among certain
immigrant groups, such as the West Indians in Stockwell and the
North Africans in Folie-Méricourt.

THE WISH TO LEAVE THE DISTRICT

Another index of the degree of contentment with a district is
the proportion of residents wishing or intending to leave it. More
cogent still is the proportion who actually do leave.

In Stockwell, the full sample of households were asked whether
they wanted to go on living in the district or would prefer to
leave it. About half said they wanted to leave, compared with a
third in an earlier survey in the London region as a whole
(Young and Willmott, 1973). To clarify people's attitudes to the
inner city, it was important to know if they wanted to move
within Inner London or out of it. Most of those who wanted to
move wished to go further out.

A further question was asked, explicitly about staying in
inner London. People were asked whether there was 'anything
at all that is keeping you from moving out of Inner London'.
About a quarter of the full sample said that they were planning
to move out of the inner city or gave other answers suggesting

they wanted to leave it. The main reasons for staying were connected with work. Thus, while the majority wanted to stay, a substantial minority of households seemed to want to leave. In an attempt to find out more about this minority, their characteristics were analysed in detail, and further interviews were carried out to see why they wanted to move, to identify the places they wanted to go to and to find out what steps if any they had already taken towards a move.

Chief among the potential movers were couples with children. But, even though their households more often contained children, fewer West Indians wanted to move, while more of the long-standing residents wanted to do so. It may well be the long-standing 'traditional' resident who feels most severely affected by the changes taking place in the inner city, including the influx of newcomers (Deakin and Ungerson, 1977).

Two years later, in 1975, a follow-up survey made it possible to check how many of those who said they wanted to move had actually done so. It turned out that about a third of these households had moved house in the period between the two surveys. More families with children had moved; they accounted for over a half of those who had left compared with a quarter of those who had stayed (Shankland et al., 1977, pp.120-2).

The second survey probed further the reasons why people wanted to move and the districts they wanted to go to. As expected, most sought better housing. Over a third were looking for a garden of their own, and a fifth wanted modern amenities. But dissatisfactions with the local environment and local people were more important than problems with housing. Altogether over a third said they wanted an area which was quieter, more peaceful or with less traffic. One in eight were looking for somewhere 'healthier' or more countrified and two-fifths simply wanted a 'nicer looking' area than Stockwell.

Among potential movers, complaints about the district were social as well as physical. Over a quarter said they wanted to live near 'friendlier' or 'nicer' neighbours or 'people more of our class', while a similar proportion wanted a better social life generally. All those with children laid emphasis on moving to an area with better play facilities. The most frequent social reason for moving, given by four people out of every ten, was to find an area with less vandalism or crime. Statements of intention apart, the evidence from the Census is that since the beginning of the century people have been leaving the inner city in their thousands, particularly families with children (Shankland et al., 1977, pp. 123-4).

The classical study of residential mobility was that of Rossi in Philadelphia; from this and from the wealth of statistical material about movers and reasons for moving in Britain, we can see how far mobility in Stockwell resembled mobility elsewhere, and the ways in which they differed (Rossi, 1955; Murie, 1974; Office of Population Censuses and Surveys, 1973). In general, households are more likely to move in their earlier than their later years.

Newly formed households predominantly move for personal reasons, mainly following marriage. For continuing households, the
main reasons are to do with housing conditions or change of job.
The younger the head and the larger the household, the higher
its inclination to move, age and size being independently related
to mobility. Where Stockwell was unusual was in the degree of
emphasis on the physical and social environment as reasons for
moving.

By contrast there is evidence that, in the rented sectors,
residential mobility is lower in the Paris agglomération than in
the French provinces, and especially low in the city of Paris
itself. This appears to be linked with the higher proportion of
older dwellings in Paris whose rent is controlled under the Law
of 1948 (Durif and Berniard, 1971). Large-scale official housing
inquiries in 1955, 1961, 1963, 1970 and 1973 included a question
on whether the household wished to move; the percentage so
wishing decreased from 27 per cent in 1955 to 21 per cent in
1973. There was a bigger fall among households who both thought
they were ill-housed and wanted to move, the proportion being
22 per cent in 1955 but only 8 per cent in 1973, suggesting that
residential mobility was decreasingly linked with the quality of
the housing itself. The housing inquiries did not pursue the
question of what the other reasons for moving might be (Durif,
1976).

Against this general background, we can compare the samples
of households with two or more children in Stockwell and Folie-
Méricourt. It must be borne in mind that households with children are more likely than other households to be overcrowded and
are also more likely to want to move. Table I.3 compares the proportion wanting to move in the two districts by occupation and
national origin of heads of household.

The table shows that households with two or more children
were about twice as likely to want to move from Folie-Méricourt
as from Stockwell, and that the wish to move was greater in
Folie-Méricourt whatever the occupation or national origin of the
household head. Within each district, national origin made more
difference than occupation, though its effect on the West Indians
of Stockwell was the reverse of that on the North Africans of
Folie-Méricourt, few of the former wishing to move but nine out
of ten of the latter.

The general difference between the two districts can probably
be attributed to the greater overcrowding in Folie-Méricourt;
this would fit in with the finding of the French national housing
inquiries that overcrowding was the factor most strongly
associated with moving and the wish to move. To test this
suggestion, Table I.4 compares the proportion wishing to move
among households with different degrees of overcrowding. The
table suggests that in both districts, among households at this
stage of life, the most overcrowded households were the most
likely to wish to move, although this was more marked in Folie-
Méricourt than in Stockwell.

Table I.3   *The wish to move by occupation and national origin of heads of*
household: households with two or more children, Stockwell
and Folie-Méricourt, 1973

	Stockwell		Folie-Méricourt	
	Percentage wishing to move	*Number in group*	*Percentage wishing to move*	*Number in group*
Occupation of head of household				
Professional and managerial	53	19	71	21
Other non-manual	47	15	71	17
Skilled manual	38	71	60	40
Semi- and unskilled manual	47	68	85	41
Unoccupied	14	29	–	–
Inadequate information	21	14	–	–
National origin of head of household				
West Indian/ North African	14	65	89	19
Other non-British/ other non-French	42	53	69	39
British/French	51	98	72	61
All households	38	216	74	119

Table I.4   *The wish to move and the number of persons per room: households*
with two or more children, Stockwell and Folie-Méricourt, 1973

	Percentage wishing to move in:			
Persons per room	Stockwell		Folie-Méricourt	
	%	*Number*	*%*	*Number*
One or less	36	106	48	15
More than one and up to 1.5	37	81	60	30
More than 1.5	46	29	84	74
Number of households		216		119

ENVIRONMENTAL DISADVANTAGE, REAL AND PERCEIVED

As we said at the beginning of the chapter, environmental disadvantage has an objective as well as a subjective component.
The objective component can, in principle, be measured with a
fair degree of accuracy. The adequacy of services such as
transport, shops, schools and doctors' surgeries and of amenities such as parks, libraries and street cleaning can be asses-
sed in terms of quantity, quality and accessibility. Although in
both areas some information was gathered on these matters,
extensive gaps remain; we lack the factual basis for a balance
sheet of objective environmental advantage and disadvantage in
the districts, compared with each other and compared with other
districts and with national and metropolitan standards.

Even if we had more objective information on different aspects
of the environment, we should still need to relate it to individual
households in the sample, to their exact location in the district
and to their particular objective needs. Finally, we should need
to go beyond these objective data and to take into account the
individual perceptions, fears, aspirations and cultural back-
grounds of respondents. Ideally we should combine objective and
subjective components of environmental disadvantage into a single index, though it is difficult to see how this could be done.
Rossi, in his Philadelphia study, showed that objective environmental disadvantages and individual subjective perception of
them seldom coincided (Rossi, 1955,Ch. III).

It is perhaps tempting, in view of these difficulties, to fall
back on the notion of 'collective' disadvantage, that is to say,
the attribution of environmental disadvantage to all the people
living in a district collectively. But this is unfair because the
disadvantage, whether in its objective or subjective aspect, is
far from being spread evenly over the whole of a district as
large as Stockwell or Folie-Méricourt. In Folie-Méricourt there
was a distinct difference between the eastern and western halves
of the quartier; even in the eastern half, where the disadvantages were concentrated, there were gradations of disadvantage
from one street or block to another. The disadvantage of the
eastern half was of little relevance to the western. People living
there, in solid nineteenth-century blocks near the Boulevard de
la République, hardly needed to see the crumbling and litter-
strewn courts a few hundred metres to the east of their homes.
Similarly, there were parts of Stockwell where the immediate
environment was extremely pleasant, with well-maintained family
houses, colourful front gardens, carefully tended triangles or
squares of grass and mature but well-pruned flowering chestnut
or lime trees. The 'oases' were the most visible examples. Apart
from the streets or housing estates that the residents might have
had to pass through on their way to their homes, there would
have been little cause for complaint in terms of the district's
physical appearance and little obtrusive awareness of its ethnic
or social character.

The data we have been able to present about likes and dislikes of the environment, about the wish to move and about
those who actually moved, make it clear that in our two inner
city districts there were substantial numbers of households on
whom the sense of environmental disadvantage weighed heavily
and many who were desperately anxious to leave it, including
some who had lived there all their lives. Despite all the limitations of the evidence, and despite the point we have just made
about local variations, the chapter confirms the force of what we
said at the outset. Though it may be difficult to measure, there
undoubtedly is such a thing as environmental disadvantage, and
in a general sense people living in the inner city districts of
Stockwell and Folie-Méricourt suffer from it more than people
living in other kinds of place.

II

HOUSEHOLD INCOMES:
The national and metropolitan
context

We now turn to more measurable kinds of disadvantage, beginning with income. Before we look at the incomes of families in
Stockwell and Folie-Méricourt, we need to provide a comparative context by drawing on government surveys for data on
household incomes in Britain and France, and in the London
Region and the Paris agglomération. This takes up the present
chapter which necessarily consists largely of statistical tables
and commentary upon them.

A person's standard of living is, broadly speaking, that of
the household in which he lives. It depends on the household's
income, and this in turn usually depends on the earnings of
the 'head of the household', to use the terminology of censuses
and surveys. What is therefore crucial for the economic level of
the household as a whole is the occupation of the head of the
household, on which hinge his earnings and the relative poverty
or affluence of its members.

These obvious points have to be made to explain why our
initial concern is not directly with income but with its main
determinant, the occupational structure, analysed in terms of
heads of households rather than of gainfully occupied men and
women. The British and French occupational structures have
been shaped by similar processes of industrial development, but
there are differences in the rates at which the two economies
have changed over from agriculture to industry and also in the
proportion of those working who are self-employed. Table II.1
illustrates the differences.

The proportion of self-employed heads of households was
higher in France than in Britain, because of the much greater
number of farmers and also of small shopkeepers. The proportion of professional and managerial heads of household was
the same in the two countries, and the proportion of 'other
non-manual' heads of household - mainly office workers and
shop assistants - somewhat higher in France. The higher proportion of manual worker heads of household in Britain was
largely due to the greater number of skilled worker heads of
household, more than twice as many as in France.

Table II.1   Occupation of heads of household

	United Kingdom 1973 %	France 1970 %
Self-employed:		
Non-manual	2 ⎫	7 ⎫
Manual	3 ⎬ 6	3 ⎬ 16
Agricultural	1 ⎭	6 ⎭
Employed:		
Professional and managerial	16	16
Other non-manual	7	11
Manual − skilled	25 ⎫	12 ⎫
semi-skilled	11 ⎬ 42	10 ⎬ 26
unskilled	6 ⎭	4 ⎭
Agricultural	1	1
Retired and unoccupied	28	30
All households	100	100

Sources: for UK, Department of Employment, 1974, p. 93, Table 40, and Central Statistical Office, 1975, p. 11, Table 1.1; for France, Bandérier, 1973, p. 16, Table 1.

HOUSEHOLD INCOMES IN BRITAIN AND FRANCE

Households derive their incomes from a variety of sources – from salaries and wages, from the profits of self-employment, from various kinds of investment and from social payments such as child benefit. In each occupational group, the 'average household' derives its income from a combination of these sources, with one source predominating. Thus obviously enough the main source of income in a household with a self-employed head was self-employment, although on average such households derived a quarter or more of their income from other sources. In the average household with a retired or unoccupied head the main source of income was social benefit, but as much as three-fifths in Britain, and two-fifths in France came from other sources. Table AI.2 (Appendix I, p.117) is an attempt to show the proportion of income from each source for households with heads having different sorts of occupation in the two countries. The table also gives an estimate of the proportion of income paid in direct taxes (income tax and social insurance contributions). In this table and later in the book, we have converted French francs to pounds sterling by using 'purchasing power parities' appropriate to the year in question (Hibbert, 1975). As Hibbert explained, since purchasing power parities are 'derived from

the comparison of prices for a representative range of goods
and services', they 'provide a more satisfactory basis for con-
verting ... to a common unit of measurement than do exchange
rates'. Here and elsewhere we show in brackets the sterling
figures for mid-1980, reflecting the increase over the period in
the British retail price index. On average, wages and salaries
contributed far less to household income in France than in
Britain, while self-employment and social benefits contributed
more. Self-employment, however, contributed only marginally
to household income except where the head of household was
himself self-employed or, to a lesser extent, if he was retired.
Social benefits contributed a relatively large proportion of the
income of all French households, least where the head of the
household was self-employed, most where the head was retired
or unoccupied (as was true for Britain) and substantially also
in households with 'other non-manual' and manual heads (which
was not true for Britain).

It is well-known that direct taxes, including social insurance
contributions, are higher in Britain than in France. In 1971 the
average household in Britain paid 16 per cent of its gross
income in direct tax and got back 9 per cent in direct social
benefit, a net loss of 7 per cent. In France in 1970 only 9 per
cent went in direct tax, while 24 per cent came back in direct
benefit, a net gain of 15 per cent. These calculations do not
take account of the effect of indirect taxation or of such indirect benefits as, for example, education. However, it is the
effects of direct taxation and benefits which are most immed-
iately experienced by people and households. Table II.2 shows
the net effect of these transfers, and also takes account, on a
simple per head basis, of the varying numbers of people in the
households receiving the incomes. To take account of a decade
of inflation, as explained in the Introduction, values at mid-
1980 are shown in brackets.

Average net income per head in France 1970 was substantially higher than in Britain 1971, but there was little difference
between the two countries for households with a 'manual' or
'other non-manual' head, which together made up half of all
households in Britain and 38 per cent in France. The biggest
difference between the countries was for households with a
self-employed head, a much larger group, as already noted, in
France than in Britain. For this group, net income per head
was over twice as much in France - £25 (mid-1980 prices: £91) -
as in Britain - £11 (1980: £37). In France, net income per head
in the self-employed group was two and a half times as high as
in those with a manual worker head, whereas in Britain there
was little difference between the two groups of households.

The high incomes of the French households with a self-
employed head largely explain why the distribution of incomes
in France was more unequal than in Britain. A closer look at
the composition of this group shows that the highest of their
incomes were concentrated among the industrial and commercial

employers and self-employed professionals who between them
headed no more than 2.1 per cent of all households, while the
others - the shopkeepers, artisans and farmers, who made up
13.2 per cent of all households in the group - had on average
incomes less than a third as large (see Table AI.3, p.118).

Table II.2　Net income per household and per head by occupation of head of
household: UK 1971, France 1970 (values at mid-1980 prices
shown in brackets)

Occupation of head of household	Net household income per week £		Number in household		Net income per head per week £	
	UK	France	UK	France	UK	France
Self-employed	37 (123)	85 (309)	3.27	3.57	11 (37)	25 (91)
Employed:						
Professional and managerial	51 (170)	64 (233)	3.13	3.36	16 (53)	19 (69)
Other non-manual	36 (120)	40 (145)	2.78	2.94	13 (43)	14 (51)
Manual	33 (110)	38 (138)	3.34	3.63	10 (33)	10 (36)
Retired and unoccupied	19 (63)	26 (95)	1.96	1.92	9 (30)	14 (51)
All households	32 (106)	47 (171)	2.89	2.98	11 (37)	16 (58)

£1 = 14.55 Fr.
Sources: for UK, Department of Employment, 1972, p. 85, Table 34; for France, Roze, 1974,
p. 32.

HOW INCOMES CHANGED IN BRITAIN AND FRANCE, 1962-70

Using government survey figures for the two countries it is
possible to see how the real incomes of different broad occupational groups of households changed over the eight years between 1962 and 1970. For this purpose, the 'self-employed' and
the 'professional and managerial' groups have been combined,
as have the 'other non-manual' and 'manual' groups. So we can
compare changes in the average income of these very broad
occupational groups over time, and changes in the ratio between
them, for the two countries. Table II.3 shows changes in weekly household income net of tax at 1962 prices and with francs
converted to pounds by the appropriate purchasing power parities.

These comparisons show a very different rate of growth in
real incomes in the two countries. They suggest that in both
countries economic growth was accompanied by a lessening

inequality between the incomes of the higher (the self-employed and professional and managerial headed households) and the lower (the manual and other non-manual). The average net income for all households increased in Britain from £22 (mid-1980 prices: £112) to £26 (1980: £132), an increase of £4 at 1962 prices (£20 at mid-1980 prices), or 18 per cent. The increase in France was from £24 (mid-1980 prices: £122) to £34 (1980: £173), or 42 per cent. The French average net household income started only a little higher than the British but ended much higher. The average annual rate of increase in Britain was 2.25 per cent a year; in France it was 5.25 per cent a year, more than twice as rapid a rate of growth.

Table II.3   Net weekly income at 1962 prices for three broad occupational groups of households: UK and France, 1962 and 1970 (values at mid-1980 prices shown in brackets)

| *Occupation of head of household* | *1962* | | | | *1970* | | | |
| | *UK* | | *France* [a] | | *UK* | | *France* [b] | |
	£	£	£	£	£	£	£	£
Self-employed and professional and managerial	36	(183)	39	(199)	40	(204)	54	(275)
Other non-manual and manual	21	(107)	19	(92)	27	(138)	28	(143)
Retired and unoccupied	12	(61)	12	(61)	14	(71)	20	(102)
All households	22	(112)	24	(122)	26	(132)	34	(173)

(a) £1 = 14.90 Fr.
(b) £1 = 14.55 Fr.
Sources: for UK, Department of Employment, 1963, p. 24ff, and Department of Employment, 1971, p. 85, Table 25; for France, Roze, 1974, p. 29, Table 11.

How did the three broad occupational groups fare over this eight-year period? In both countries the combined self-employed and professional and managerial group had gained less than the average. In Britain their annual rate of increase was 1.37 per cent compared with the average of 2.25 per cent for all incomes. In France their annual rate of increase was 4.75 per cent compared with the average of 5.25 per cent for all incomes. In both countries, on the other hand, the combined 'other non-manual' and manual categories gained at rates well above the average, 3.62 per cent a year in Britain, and 7.00 per cent a year in France. Households with a retired or unoccupied head of household gained slightly less than the average in Britain, with a rate of increase of 2.12 per cent a year, but in France these households gained most of all, with an increase of 8.37 per cent

a year.
   The more rapid increase, in both countries, of other non-
manual and manual incomes compared with self-employed, professional and managerial incomes must mean a reduction of
inequality. Table II.4 shows the ratio between the incomes of
these two groups for both countries at both dates. The ratio
between the two was lower, that is to say less unequal, in
Britain than in France at both dates. However, the French
ratio moved a little faster in the direction of less inequality.

*Table II.4   Ratio of net incomes of 'self-employed, professional and
           managerial' households to those of 'other non-manual and manual'
           households: UK and France, 1962 and 1970*

	1962	1970	Change 1962-70
UK	1.7	1.5	−0.2
France	2.2	1.9	−0.3

Sources: for UK, Department of Employment, 1963, pp. 24ff, and Department of
Employment, 1971, p. 85, Table 25; for France, Roze, 1974, p. 29, Table 11.

   Another indication of the reduction of income inequality over
the period is the evolution, in real terms, of statutory minimum
welfare levels set by the governments of the two countries. In
Britain, rates of supplementary benefit provide such a level -
indeed they are commonly if misleadingly referred to as 'the
official poverty line'. In France, the SMIC (salaire minimum
interprofessionnel de croissance) or statutory minimum wage
level is a measure with a comparable history though it measures
not poverty but low pay.
   Supplementary benefit, formerly called national assistance,
was raised each year after 1948, at first to keep up with rising
prices, but from 1959 to take account also of increases in average earnings. The SMIC, earlier called SMIG (salaire minimum
interprofessionnel garanti) has also been raised each year
since its inception in 1950. It too has evolved from its first
function of keeping up with prices to taking account of increasing real average earnings.
   The real value of supplementary benefit in 1971 was 24 per
cent higher than in 1963, an average increase of 3 per cent a
year. This increase was more than the average increase of 2.25
per cent for all household incomes in Britain. Between 1962 and
1970, the real value of SMIG rose by 45 per cent, or 5.6 per
cent a year, again more than the average household increase in
France of 5.25 per cent a year.
   To sum up the changes between 1962 and 1970, in both
countries there was over the period a marked increase in real
household incomes, some decrease in inequality and a decrease,
in absolute terms, in poverty and low pay.

OCCUPATION AND INCOME IN LONDON AND PARIS

We now change focus from national to metropolitan comparisons.
Table II.5 compares the occupational structure of the two
countries, the two metropolitan areas (Greater London and the
Paris agglomération) and the two inner cities (Inner London
and Paris itself). This time the figures are not of heads of
households but of economically active males as enumerated by
the Census.

In both countries, the proportion of professional and managerial men was higher in the metropolitan area than nationally.
This was most marked in France, where the proportion of them
in the inner city of Paris was double that in France as a whole.
This shows both the concentration of the more highly paid
occupations in the French capital, and also the greater tendency
in France for holders of these positions to live within the
boundaries of the inner city rather than further afield. The
opposite tendency can be seen in London, where more professional and managerial males lived outside than inside the
boundaries of Inner London. There were, correspondingly,
more male manual workers living in Inner London (52 per cent)
than in Greater London as a whole (47 per cent), while the
opposite was true of inner Paris, with only 40 per cent male
manual workers, compared to 49 per cent in the agglomération.
Inner London had the same proportion of male skilled manual
workers as Greater London (27 per cent) but more semi-skilled
and unskilled (25 per cent compared to 20 per cent). Inner
Paris had fewer in all three manual worker categories, the
deficiency of skilled workers being the greatest. All these differences reflect differing patterns of residential movement and
urban development, as well as of the occupational structure
itself.

It is partly the higher proportion of professional and managerial men that accounts for the average household income
being well above that of the rest of the country, both in Greater
London and in the Paris region. In 1971, average household
income per week before tax was £43.80 (mid-1980 prices:
£145.59) in Greater London, compared to £38.48 (1980: £127.91)
in Britain generally (14 per cent higher) (Department of Employment 1972, p.14, Table 56). In 1970, average household income
per week before direct taxes or benefits was £41 (mid-1980
prices: £149.08) in the Paris region compared to £26 (1980:
£94.54) in the rest of France (58 per cent higher) (Bandérier,
1973, p.19, Table 4). Clearly the metropolitan income differential was much greater for Paris than for London. In the Paris
region, in addition to the effect of an occupational structure
with a higher than average proportion of the more highly paid
occupations, households with heads in all occupational categories had higher incomes than their counterparts elsewhere in
the country. For households with a self-employed head, income
was 48 per cent higher in the Paris region than in the rest of

Table II.5   Occupation of economically active males: UK, Greater London, Inner London, 1971; France, Paris agglomération, Paris, 1968

Occupation of economically active males	UK 1971 %	Greater London 1971 %	Inner London 1971 %	France 1968 %	Paris agglomération 1968 %	Paris 1968 %
Professional and managerial (a)	23	27	23	17	30	34
Self-employed non-professional	9 (b)	6	5	19 (c)	6	8
Other non-manual	12	16	15	9	12	14
Skilled manual	33	27	27	25	25	19
Semi-skilled manual	14	13	15	21	17	15
Unskilled manual	8	7	10	8	7	6
Other (d)	1	4	5	1	3	4

(a) Including self-employed professional
(b) Including 2 per cent farmers
(c) Including 12 per cent farmers
(d) In UK, armed forces and unstated; in France, army and police (other than officers)
Sources: UK, 1971 Census; France, 1968 Census

France. With a cadre supérieur head it was 25 per cent higher, with a cadre moyen head 27 per cent higher, with an 'other non-manual' head 19 per cent, with a manual worker head 32 per cent, and with a retired or unoccupied head 50 per cent higher.

Some items in the cost of living in Paris were also higher, rents in particular. In 1973, rent per square metre was 47 per cent higher in the agglomération than nationally, and as much as 75 per cent higher in Paris itself (Durif, 1975). However, an inquiry into retail prices in 1971 found that public transport actually cost less in Paris than nationally, while the cost of all items (other than rent, furniture and insurances) was only about 4 per cent higher than nationally (Picard, 1972).

In London, the great majority of public sector employees and many private sector employees receive an addition to their salaries and wages known as London Weighting to compensate for the extra costs involved. A report by the Pay Board in 1974 recommended that those working in Inner London should receive an extra £400 a year, of which £141 was to compensate for extra housing costs, £73 for the cost of travel to work, £81 for other costs and £105 for 'wear and tear' (Pay Board, 1974).

This chapter, in setting the context for examining income poverty in Stockwell and Folie-Méricourt, has shown that the average net household income per head was higher in France than in Britain, but that for households with manual worker or 'other non-manual' worker heads it was much the same in both countries. The big difference was for households with a self-employed head – 16 per cent of all households in France, only 6 per cent in England – whose net income per head was £25 (mid-1980 prices: £91) a week in France, only £11 (1980: £37) in England.

These French self-employed people were largely responsible for the greater inequality of household incomes in France. They have, however, been diminishing in numbers; and the ratio of the net incomes of 'self-employed, professional and managerial households' to those of 'other non-manual and manual households' also diminished between 1962 and 1970. Income inequality was greater in France, but over this period was decreasing rather faster in France than in Britain. Supplementary benefit in Britain and SMIC, the French statutory minimum wage level, both increased over this period more than average household incomes increased in Britain and France respectively.

At the metropolitan level of comparison, we found that while in Greater London incomes were 14 per cent higher than in the rest of Britain, in the Paris region they were 58 per cent higher than in the rest of France. This was partly because of the higher proportion in the metropolitan region of households with heads in the higher-income occupations, and partly because at every occupational level, incomes were higher in Paris than elsewhere.

With such variations as these in mind, we can now look more

closely at the contrasted patterns of jobs and of household incomes in the two inner city districts.

III

INCOME INEQUALITY AND POVERTY:
Stockwell and Folie-Méricourt

We begin this chapter with descriptions of some families. Although our prime concern is with household income, some
other detail is given to round out the picture. Several of the
families are in poverty, on the definition given later in this
chapter, but they are not among the most heavily disadvantaged, for a number of whom there are details in Chapter VI,
on multiple disadvantage.

The families cover a range of different occupational groups
and with different national origins. We start with those most
prone to poverty - the households with an 'unoccupied' head -
and finish with the best-off - the professional and managerial
people. As explained in the Introduction, all these households
included two or more children, and there were no households
with heads who were self-employed or employed by the State.
All figures for incomes and rents are at 1973 values, with
values at mid-1980 prices shown in brackets.

Mrs Minton, a twenty-six-year-old mother in Stockwell, had
no job and no husband. She lived with three children aged
six, five and under a year, in a council flat for which she paid
£3.13 (mid-1980 prices: £8.89) a week, rebated from £6.00
(1980: £17.04). The flat had two bedrooms, and was on the first
floor of a post-war block. She had previously lived with her
mother, but there had not been enough space. The council was
supposed to have done the place up before she moved in, she
said, but it had never done so. She told the interviewer that
she had no special problems, but she would have liked a ground-
floor flat to save her pulling the pram up and down stairs. She
had lived in the district between ten and fifteen years, but
said 'I don't really know what a neighbourhood is'. Her parents
lived just round the corner and she had friends within ten
minutes' walk. She thought there was not enough for the
children to do in the district, nothing to interest them and
keep them out of trouble: 'Teenagers just explode into vio-
lence.' She complained too about lack of jobs. She would not
herself have minded leaving, but would stay because her boy-
friend did not want to move. She had had no holiday in the last
year; the last time she had been out for an evening had been
more than a month previously, and she had no leisure activities
(out of a list of ten) in the past month. Her income was £15.50
(1980: £44.02) supplementary benefit and £1.80 (1980: £5.11)
in family allowances.

Mr Awolowo, a Nigerian and also living in Stockwell, was a

full-time student at a technical college, aged thirty-three. His
wife, aged twenty-nine, worked as a cleaner at the Shell building on the South Bank. They had two small boys aged five and
three. They had a fourth-floor four-roomed inter-war council
flat, for which they paid rent of £5.40 (1980: £15.34) a week,
not rebated. Previously the family had lived in one room,
rented furnished. Mrs Awolowo would have liked central heating
and a larger kitchen. There was no lift, and the neighbours
gave noisy parties. The pair had lived in the district between
five and ten years but did not know anybody. They found it
convenient for transport and shopping, but they disliked the
break-ins and the rubbish left around on the estate. The wife
could not let the children go outside because of the stairs, and
the other children round there were 'rough'. 'You can't bring
up children when you are on top of a house like this.' However,
they intended to stay because it was close to her work and her
husband's college. They had taken no holiday in the previous
year; during the past month both had been to the cinema and
had read books; Mr Awolowo had had a meal at a restaurant,
done home repairs and taken part in sport. Their main problem
was low income. The wife earned £21 (1980: £59.64) a week, and
received £0.90 (1980: £2.56) family allowance.

Mrs O'Brien, who had been born in Stockwell, was a twenty-
six-year-old mother, separated, with son of six and daughter
of two. Her husband could not be traced; he had contributed
nothing for eight years. She lived in two rooms rented furnished and paid a rent of £5.32 (1980: £15.11). She shared the
use of a bath and WC. She was depending on her present home
being pulled down so that she could be rehoused - it had been
scheduled for demolition for about three years. She had not
worked for eight and a half years - supplementary benefit was
more than she could earn on a part-time job.

> 'I didn't believe in working when they was small - there
> was enough to do to look after them anyway. I'd think
> about working if I had a nice place - something to work for-
> but not for this. When they're both at school and we have
> a decent place - then I shall work. A nice home is the most
> important thing in life, because it takes the tension out of
> everything else. You can put up with a lot of other troubles
> if you've got a nice home. I was dead unlucky to get a man
> who was tight with his money. I suppose I'm lucky in a way.
> I've got my family - my Mum and my sister - so I'm not on
> my own. I get on better with Mum now I've got a place of
> my own. She's one in a million.'

Her mother lived nearby. Mrs O'Brien also had friends
amongst the mothers whose children attended playgroup and
among the women whom she met at the launderette. The women
visited each other and sometimes her neighbour from upstairs
would call on her in the evening to have a cup of tea and watch

television after the children had fallen asleep. She said that
there should be crossings on the main road, particularly
opposite the park and the school. There was nowhere for the
children to play; the roads made it unsafe. It was, she said,
now a rough area, with lots of pubs, drunks and bottles thrown
in the street. It was getting worse, with more and more traffic.
She would have liked to move, but felt that to do so she would
need to have a husband with her, 'someone to give support
which I haven't got'. She had had no holiday in the year and
no leisure activities in the previous month except meeting
friends. She received £17.50 (1980: £49.70) supplementary
benefit plus £0.90 (1980: £2.56) family allowance.

Mr Vasco, in Folie-Méricourt, was Spanish, a forty-four-year-
old foundry worker (semi-skilled) with a wife of forty-two and
three sons aged seven, five and two. Mr Vasco had left school
at the age of nine and his wife was illiterate. They lived in one
small room, with no bath and an outside WC. Mrs Vasco had a
varicose vein in her leg; Mr Vasco had a spot on his lung, a
crooked spine and two fractured toes, badly set. The two elder
boys had trouble with tonsils and adenoids; the youngest had
been born yellow and had had all his blood changed. Mr Vasco
earned £32.48 (1980: £92.24) a week and his wife £2.05 (1980:
£5.82); and they received £9.03 (1980: £25.65) in family allowances. They had been away for four weeks' holiday during the
previous year.

Mr Pochard, in Folie-Méricourt, a twenty-eight-year-old shoe-
moulder (semi-skilled) had a wife of twenty-five and two sons
aged eight and three. They lived rent-free in two tiny rooms.
They wanted to move, because their home was too small and
uncomfortable, but they did not like the idea of living in a
suburb. Mrs Pochard would not go out at night for fear of being attacked by Algerians. The building in which they lived
belonged to the owner of the factory where Mr Pochard worked,
and payment for acting as caretaker was included in his wages
of £32.48 (1980: £92.24) a week. They received £3.38 (1980:
£9.60) a week family allowance. They had a car. Mr Pochard
had had four weeks' holiday in the previous year, and his wife
eight weeks' holiday at her parents' farm in Brittany.

Mr Pidal, a West Indian in Stockwell, was a thirty-eight-year-
old general labourer at Gatwick Airport, with a thirty-five-year-old
wife working part-time on assembly work at a plastics factory
in Vauxhall, and two children – a daughter aged eleven and a
son aged thirteen. They were buying their seven-roomed flat,
paying £14 (1980: £39.76) a week mortgage. They would have
liked an extra bathroom and WC. They liked the area: 'It is
nice and quiet, and the park is just across the road.' They took
no holiday and their only leisure activities were home repairs
and meeting friends. Mr Pidal earned £32.50 (1980: £92.30) a
week; his wife earned £10.50 (1980: £29.82) and received £0.90
(1980: £2.56) family allowance.

Mr Figuera, a Spaniard living in Stockwell, was a forty-one-

year-old waiter working in Soho, with a thirty-four-year-old
wife, two sons aged fourteen and thirteen and a daughter of
eleven. They lived in a three-roomed flat rented unfurnished
from a property company for £5.70 (1980: £16.19) a week.
They wanted to move because they were overcrowded and
suffered from damp and rats; they were on the Council's housing list. They found the area convenient for transport but
unattractive to look at. They thought the schools were good.
They had friends within walking distance. They had gone back
to Spain for a holiday during the year. During the previous
month they had been out for a drive and met friends; Mr Figuera
had also been to a pub and Mrs Figuera had done home decorations and read a book. Mr Figuera earned £23.00 (1980: £65.32)
a week and they had £1.90 (1980: £5.40) family allowance.

Mr Benson, born in Peckham, was a fifty-three-year-old
electrician's mate with a thirty-seven-year-old wife who worked
as a telephone order clerk at a greengrocer's shop, a son of
eight and a daughter of three. They lived in a first-floor five-
roomed council flat in Stockwell for which they paid £11.92
(1980: £33.85) a week – they had only just moved in and hadn't
applied for a rent rebate, though Mr Benson said the expense
was 'terrible'. They thought the council was not concerned
enough about its tenants, but that it was a good district for
bringing up children, as the schools and church were near: 'My
daughter mixes with the right kind.' However, it was overcrowded – 'more like a concrete jungle' – and there was too much
vandalism. They would stay, though, because of his job. Mr
Benson suffered from nervous anxiety, and in the previous
twelve months had been off work during a four weeks' spell in
hospital as well as off sick for a further ten weeks. They had
been on a short holiday – less than a week – and had had no
leisure activities in the previous month other than going to a
pub. Mr Benson earned £29 (1980: £82.36) a week and Mrs
Benson £21 (1980: £59.64), with £0.90 (1980: £2.56) family
allowance.

Mr Medalia, Portuguese, was a forty-three-year-old locksmith-
welder with a wife of the same age, a daughter of eighteen working as a sewing-machinist in a toy factory, and four sons aged
sixteen, fifteen, thirteen and eleven. They lived in two rooms
in Folie-Méricourt, with no bath, at a rent of £7.69 (1980: £21.84)
a week; they wanted to move because they were severely overcrowded. Mrs Medalia had had a hysterectomy and two bladder
stone operations; she had a pension of unrecorded amount from
Portugal because of head pains resulting from work in a factory.
Mr Medalia had a liver complaint. They had had four weeks'
holiday. They had a car in which they went for drives and
visited friends, and they went to a café or restaurant, the wife
occasionally, Mr Medalia within the previous week. He earned
£39.32 (1980: £111.67) a week, the daughter of eighteen earned
£17.09 (1980: £48.54) and they received £8.89 (1980: £25.25)
a week in family allowance.

Mr Garoult, Paris-born and living in Folie-Méricourt, was a twenty-eight-year-old cook on the 'Train Bleu' (the nightly wagon-lit train running from the Gare du Lyon to the Riviera). He had a twenty-five-year-old wife who worked in a café, a son aged seven and daughters aged five and two. They lived in three rooms, for which they paid £8.55 (1980: £24.28) a week. Because they needed more space they wanted to move, but not to a suburb. They had a car and their own house in the country, where they took a six-week holiday. The husband earned £59.84 (1980: £169.95) a week, and the wife £17.09 (1980: £48.54), and they received £6.84 (1980: £19.43) a week in family allowances.

Mr McCracken, born in Eire and now living in Stockwell, was a forty-three-year-old maintenance fitter working for the Gas Board with a thirty-six-year-old wife working as a part-time cleaner at a nearby school, a son of sixteen at school, four other sons (fifteen, ten, eight and four) and two daughters (twelve and five). They lived in a seven-roomed council-owned terraced house for which they paid £8.33 (1980: £23.66) a week; previously they had had a rent rebate, but had lost it with changed circumstances. They did not like the area, as there were 'a lot of houses closed up all around', and the repairs on the house needed to be finished – the window frames were poor.

They had lived in the district more than twenty years but did not feel there was a local neighbourhood to which they belonged, and they had no friends within ten minutes' walk. Stockwell was central for getting to work, and convenient for shops, buses and tubes. But they disliked the empty houses, and the type of people who lived in the street; there were no playing fields; the air was polluted by the heavy lorries; it was getting worse – everything had been 'allowed to go to rack and ruin'. People dumped rubbish in the old houses and the children lit fires in them – 'we had to get the fire brigade'. However, they intended to stay; Mr McCracken thought it would be too inconvenient and difficult to get work elsewhere, and Mrs McCracken preferred to stay in the town – she did not like the country. Mr McCracken suffered from a slipped disc, which limited his activity. He had been to a pub; they had both done home repairs and met friends. The daughter of fifteen had been away from home on a four weeks' holiday; she had been out for the evening in the previous week, and in the previous month had been to the cinema, gone to a restaurant, been to a pub, read a book, watched sport and met friends. Mr McCracken earned £47.50 (1980: £134.90) a week, his wife earned £16.50 (1980: £46.86), and they received £2.90 (1980: £8.24) in family allowances.

Mr Twigg, a West Indian in Stockwell, was a thirty-two-year-old carpenter, with a thirty-one-year-old wife working as a part-time cleaner and with two sons aged nine and four. They lived in a first-floor four-roomed inter-war council flat for which they paid £5.42 (1980: £15.39) a week; they had been on the

housing list for five years. They would have liked a dining
room or larger kitchen that they could all eat in together.
Mr Twigg would not let his children go out much - 'The children playing outside don't really play. They are too aggressive;
they fight and hit each other.' He would have liked to move but
would stay, because he did not want to interrupt his child's
schooling. They had taken no holiday in the previous year, but
he went out each week for judo and had also been to a pub and
met friends; Mrs Twigg had been for a drive. Mr Twigg earned
£37.50 (1980: £106.50) a week and Mrs Twigg £10.50 (1980:
£29.82) with £0.90 (1980: £2.56) family allowance.

Mr Delors, French-born and a thirty-nine-year-old petrol
station attendant with a thirty-five-year-old wife, three
daughters (fourteen, seven and six) and a son (ten), was living in Folie-Méricourt in three rooms at £8.72 (1980: £24.76) a
week. They had a car and had been for a drive in the previous
week, and they had taken one week's holiday. Mr Delors earned
£29.06 (1980: £82.58) a week, with £11.11 (1980: £31.55)
family allowances.

Mr O'Connor was a thirty-five-year-old Irish-born bank
messenger in Stockwell. He had a thirty-two-year-old wife, who
worked as a part-time canteen assistant in a factory at Camberwell, and a son aged ten and a daughter aged six. They lived
in a four-roomed terraced house, rented private unfurnished
for £3.61 (1980: £10.25) a week. They expected the rent would
be raised, probably to £6.00 (1980: £17.04) a week, as they
had just had a bathroom put in. They disliked the area - the
youngsters were out of control, threw bottles against the wall.
They had no friends or relatives living near. They thought
the district would have been better if it had been 'less populated'. They would have liked to move to somewhere in the
country but knew that if they left their flat they would never
get another one. They had taken no holiday during the year.
Mr O'Connor's only leisure activity had been going to a pub;
Mrs O'Connor had done home decorations and read a book. Mr
O'Connor earned £21.00 (1980: £59.64) a week and his wife
£8.50 (1980: £24.14), with £0.90 (1980: £2.56) family allowance.

Mr Julie, in Folie-Méricourt and French-born, was a fifty-
year-old head of an accounts department with a forty-five-year-
old wife doing a part-time clerical job and two daughters aged
fifteen and twelve, living in three rooms with no bath or hot
water, paying £3.42 (1980: £9.71) a week. They wanted to
leave because it was too small and lacked amenities. Mrs Julie
also disliked the area because of the immigrants. She had left
school at seventeen, he at twenty. They had no car and he had
had no holiday, though she had been away for a fortnight. He
earned £42.74 (1980: £121.38) a week and she £10.26 (1980:
£29.14) with £3.57 (1980: £10.14) a week family allowance.

Mr Boursault, also French-born, was a thirty-nine-year-old
marketing director with a thirty-nine-year-old wife, a daughter
of ten and two sons, nine and four, living in a five-roomed

flat, for which they paid £18.80 (1980: £53.39) a week. They would have liked to move, because of difficulties with their neighbours over the children. Mr Boursault had been brought up in the district. Mrs Boursault had friends there, and liked the central position, but she disliked the lack of green space, the noise and the traffic. She had finished full-time education at 22, he at 25. They had a car and a house in the country. He took five weeks' holiday there, and she was there for fourteen weeks during the summer. In the previous week they had been to a restaurant, taken part in sport, gone to a concert and been to the cinema. He earned £118 (1980: £335) a week, with £8.55 (1980: £24.28) from another source (unspecified) and £5.81 (1980: £16.50) family allowance.

Mr Janpat, Indian-born and living in Stockwell, was a forty-five-year-old restaurant manager with a thirty-seven-year-old wife who worked full-time as an office secretary in Westminster. They had a six-year-old daughter and a four-year-old son, and lived in part of a terraced house rented furnished from a property company, for which they paid £6.00 (1980: £17.04) a week. They were moving shortly to the flat downstairs, which had two more rooms, for £10.00 (1980: £28.40) a week. At the time of the interview they had only one bedroom and shared a WC with three other families. Their car had recently been stolen. Another night when Mr Janpat was home late from work, he had been beaten up and had to have ten stitches in his head; three teenage boys were caught and given a jail sentence for this. Mrs Janpat said she had to work as they could not make ends meet. The traffic outside was too heavy for the children to be allowed out safely, but she could not keep them in all the time. Though the rooms were supposed to be furnished, there was no proper furniture and they had had to buy everything. They had taken two weeks' holiday, and in the previous month had gone to a restaurant, done home repairs, read a book and met friends. Mr Janpat earned £23.00 (1980: £65.32) a week and his wife £21.00 (1980: £59.64), with £0.90 (1980: £2.56) family allowance.

Mr Darwin (Stockwell, English-born) was a twenty-nine-year-old executive marketing manager for an oil company with a twenty-six-year-old wife working as a secretary with a computing agency. They had three sons, a one-year-old and one-month-old twins, and lived in a six-roomed terraced house which they owned, paying £12.48 (1980: £35.44) a week for the mortgage and rates. They would have liked a few more rooms and a garage. They felt the area to be a neighbourhood - 'The Oval' - with small shops and good neighbours, many of them people in similar circumstances to themselves. 'It's friendly and it's very central; one hasn't got to commute for hours.' They had friends living within ten minutes' walk and had met them socially during the previous week. They thought the streets should be cleaned more often - there was litter in them all the time. They also thought the district needed better parking

facilities and more open space for children to play; the lorries
should be excluded, the housing should be improved, there
should be less concrete and tarmac. They had been abroad for
their holiday, for more than four weeks. In the previous month
they had been to the theatre and to a restaurant, and both had
read books and met friends; Mr Darwin had been to a pub, done
home repairs and taken part in sport. Mrs Darwin had been away
from work for sixteen weeks while expecting her twins. Mr
Darwin finished his education in his twenties, she at eighteen.
He earned £75 (1980: £213) a week and she £19.50 (1980: £55.38),
plus £1.90 (1980: £5.40) family allowance.

UNEQUAL INCOMES

Household incomes in the two areas depended not only on the
occupation of the head of the household, but also on whether
wives were working as well as husbands, in spite of having two
or more children to look after. In some households there were
other earners as well as husbands and wives. Every household
drew social benefits in the form of family allowances, and sometimes other benefits as well. How much each of these sources
contributed is set out in Tables AI.4 and AI.5 (pp.119, 120) which
are based only on those households where the husband was
earning and where there was adequate information; these comprised two-thirds of the Stockwell and 87 per cent of the Folie-
Méricourt households. For such households, husband's earnings
contributed the same proportion, 70 per cent, in both study
areas, and the total household income was much the same in
both, £55.97 (mid-1980 prices: £158.98) in Stockwell and £53.91
(1980: £153.10) in Folie-Méricourt. Wife's earnings were higher
in Stockwell,and social benefits in Folie-Méricourt. The apparent
slight advantage of the Stockwell households would disappear
if direct taxes were deducted from families' incomes in both
places.

Professional and managerial husbands in Stockwell were earning on average about £23 (1980: £65) a week less than their
opposite numbers in Folie-Méricourt. They were also paying
more income tax (though this is not shown in the Appendix
table) and getting less in social benefits. Their average gross
household income was £32 (1980: £91) a week less than that of
the equivalent Folie-Méricourt households. 'Other non-manual'
husbands were earning less in Folie-Méricourt than in Stockwell,
but the difference was more than made up by the social benefits they received, which provided nearly a fifth of their
household incomes, compared with only a twenty-fifth of the
equivalent Stockwell household incomes. Stockwell manual
worker husbands, skilled and semi- and unskilled, earned more
than such workers were earning in Folie-Méricourt, and their
household incomes were also appreciably higher, the earnings
of the wives and others more than making up for the lower
social benefits they received.

In both places, the national origin of the head of household
also made a difference to household income, especially to the
amount contributed by wives when they were earning as well
as their husbands. West Indian husbands were earning much
more than North African husbands. West Indian wives were
contributing an exceptionally high proportion of household
income, and North African wives none at all, the small amount
shown in the Appendix table being due to a Tunisian husband's
French wife, who was a rather high earner. North African
households derived an especially high proportion of their income
from social benefits, mainly because they had more children.
'Other non-British' and 'other non-French' households were
somewhat more similar to each other, the former owing more to
'other earnings', the latter to 'social benefits'. In neither group
were household incomes anywhere near those of the British-
born and French-born households, the figure for the latter
being boosted by the high earnings and larger numbers of professional and managerial households in the Folie-Méricourt sample.

The differences in the figures for wife's earnings were due
partly to differences in the proportion of wives working, and
partly to the amounts they earned, as shown in Table AI.6
(p.121). More professional and managerial wives were working
in Stockwell than in Folie-Méricourt, but the amounts earned by
the Folie-Méricourt professional and managerial wives (more of
whom worked full-time) were higher than those earned by their
Stockwell counterparts, which were not much more than those
earned by the wives of skilled manual workers. A similar pattern was evident among 'other non-manual' wives in the two
areas. The working wives of manual workers on the other hand
had substantially more in Stockwell than in Folie-Méricourt.

Of the national origin groups in Stockwell, West Indian wives
stood out, with the highest proportion working and a high contribution per wife. As explained earlier, the figure for North
African wives in Table AI.6 results from a solitary instance of
a French woman married to a Tunisian and, in reality, the contrast between West Indian and North African wives was total.
The average amount contributed by French working wives was
higher than for their British opposite numbers, since all the
high-earning professional and managerial wives in Folie-
Méricourt were French. The figures for 'all households' show
more wives working in Stockwell, but the contribution per
working wife was similar in the two areas.

West Indians and North Africans each have their own distinctive cultural patterns, the one encouraging, the other
totally discouraging mothers of young children from going to
work. Another cultural factor which affected the prosperity of
the different national origin groups was the number of children per household; this is shown in Table III.1.

The larger number of children to be maintained out of household income reduced the advantage given by the high propor-

tion of working wives in the West Indian households, as well
as adding to the difficulties of combining work with parenthood.
The North African households, with low average earnings, were
further impoverished by their large number of children, though
it increased their share of the liberal French family allowances.

*Table III.1   Number of children per household by national origin of head of
household: households with two or more children, husbands
earning, Stockwell and Folie-Méricourt, 1973*

Stockwell		Folie-Méricourt	
West Indian	3.94	North African	4.39
Other non-British	2.55	Other non-French	2.76
British	2.52	French	2.78
All	2.97	All	3.03

The prosperity or poverty of a household can be measured
by its income net of housing costs 'per equivalent adult'. The
idea is to allow for household composition by giving specified
'weights' to household members. In this comparative study we
used for both places the weightings adopted in the Folie-
Méricourt enquiry; head of household, 1.0; other adults. 0.7;
school-age children, 0.5. Table III.2 shows the net income per
equivalent adult in different occupational groups and those of
different national origin. At the top of the occupational scale,
the professional and managerial households of Folie-Méricourt
were far better off than those of Stockwell. This lifted the
average figure for households of French national origin above
the British. But it did not quite bring the figure for all Folie-
Méricourt households up to that for all Stockwell households,
which was helped by the relative prosperity of the West Indians
compared to the North Africans.

Viewed in a wider perspective, the figures in Table III.2
show that there was more income inequality between the households of Folie-Méricourt than between those of Stockwell, and
that this was true both for occupational groups and for national
origin groups. The point can be brought out by the ratios
between the highest and lowest occupational group and the
highest and lowest national origin group in the two places, as
is shown in Table III.3.

POVERTY IN STOCKWELL AND FOLIE-MÉRICOURT

Before we present our data on poverty in the two study areas,
we need to clarify how we are defining the term in this book, a
matter already touched on in the Introduction. We needed to
decide upon a level below which people would be judged to be

Table III.2   Household weekly income net of housing costs per equivalent
              adult, by occupation and national origin of head of household:
              households with two or more children, husbands earning,
              Stockwell and Folie-Méricourt, 1973 (values at mid-1980 prices
              shown in brackets)

	Stockwell	Folie-Méricourt (£1 = 13.50 Fr.)
Occupation of head of household		
Professional and managerial	£18.54 (52.65)	£27.88 (79.17)
Other non-manual	12.70 (36.07)	11.35 (32.23)
Skilled manual	16.80 (47.71)	14.23 (40.41)
Semi- and unskilled manual	12.77 (36.27)	10.75 (30.53)
National origin of head of household		
West Indian/North African	14.30 (40.61)	9.91 (28.14)
Other non-British/other non-French	13.59 (38.60)	12.58 (35.73)
British/French	15.92 (45.21)	17.35 (49.27)
All households	14.93 (42.40)	14.62 (41.52)

Table III.3   Ratio between the income per equivalent adult of the highest and
              lowest occupational and national origin groups of household:
              households with two or more children, husbands earning,
              Stockwell and Folie-Méricourt, 1973

	Stockwell	Folie-Méricourt
Ratio between highest and lowest occupational group	1.45	2.59
Ratio between highest and lowest national origin group	1.17	1.75

'in poverty', and a level that could be applied to both samples.
We followed the Lambeth Inner Area Study and other British
researchers in taking as our starting point a figure 20 per cent
above the level of supplementary benefits then current for a
single person: £8.58 at the time of the survey in 1973, the
equivalent of £24.37 at mid-1980 prices. Since housing costs
are usually paid in full by the Supplementary Benefits Commission in Britain, and since there is in any case an argument for
assessing income disadvantage in terms of disposable income
after housing costs have been deducted, we deducted them from
the household income. So a person living alone was defined as
'in poverty' if his or her net income, after deduction of housing
costs, was less than £8.58 a week. In order to provide a measure of more severe economic disadvantage, we drew a second
line, £5.72 or two-thirds of the poverty level (1980: £16.24),
and judged the person living alone with less than this as in
'severe poverty'.

In allowing for other household members and calculating the
income 'per equivalent adult' for each household, we did not for
this comparative study follow the complex set of weightings used
by the Supplementary Benefits Commission (which, against the
1.0 for the head of household, allowed 0.63 for a spouse, 0.80
for any other adult dependant and varying amounts from 0.29
to 0.61 for children, according to their age). Instead we
adopted the simplified weightings used in Folie-Méricourt (as in
many other French studies) which we have cited earlier in the
chapter.

We converted our two Stockwell 'poverty lines' to Folie-
Méricourt by applying the 'purchasing power parities', mentioned in the previous chapter, to allow for differences in the
'cost of living' in Britain and France. This gave 1973 figures of
116 Fr. per equivalent adult as the 'poverty line' in Folie-
Méricourt and 77 Fr. as the 'severe poverty line'. To facilitate
comparison we have throughout the book presented the Folie-
Méricourt incomes in pounds rather than francs.

Table III.4 shows, for the different occupational groups,
which here include (for Stockwell) the 'unoccupied' and 'inadequate information' groups, the proportion of our samples of
Stockwell and Folie-Méricourt households who fell below the
poverty line and below the severe poverty line, defined in the
way we have just explained.

The table shows that, on these definitions, there was more
poverty and more severe poverty in Stockwell than in Folie-
Méricourt, and that it was highly concentrated in households
with an unoccupied head, of which there were none in the Folie-
Méricourt sample. Of the twenty-nine households in the Stockwell sample so classified, twenty-eight were in poverty, including seventeen in severe poverty. In eighteen of the twenty-nine
'unoccupied' households, the head of household was a lone
mother and in the remaining eleven, a male student or trainee
or a man unemployable through disability.

Table III.4   Proportion of households in 'poverty' and 'severe poverty', by occupation of head of household: households with two or more children, Stockwell and Folie-Méricourt, 1973

Occupation of head of household	Stockwell			Folie-Méricourt		
	'Poverty' %	'Severe poverty' %	Number of households in group	'Poverty' %	'Severe poverty' %	Number of households in group
Professional and managerial	5	0	19	0	0	21
Other non-manual	47	7	15	35	0	17
Skilled manual	13	1	71	5	0	40
Semi- and unskilled manual	31	16	68	29	7	41
Unoccupied	97	59	29	–	–	–
Inadequate information	0	0	14	–	–	–
All households	31	13	216	17	3	119

Lone mothers - those who, for a variety of reasons, have no husband in the household - have been shown in other surveys to be vulnerable to poverty. In Stockwell most of them, but not all, were in the 'unoccupied' group. But having a job did not guarantee that they were out of poverty; of eight who were working, four were in poverty as we have defined it, two in severe poverty. The Stockwell sample had more lone mothers (12 per cent) than the Folie-Méricourt sample (5 per cent). Of the six lone mothers in the Folie-Méricourt sample, five were working and were not in poverty. The sixth, an unemployed hairdresser, was in severe poverty.

At the time of the survey there was relatively little unemployment in either of the two study areas. In Stockwell, of the seventeen households where the husband was unemployed or off sick, thirteen were in poverty, including nine in severe poverty. There were also households where, although there was a husband and he was working, he did not earn enough to keep the household out of poverty. There were twenty-one of these in the Stockwell sample, two of them in severe poverty; there were seventeen in the Folie-Méricourt sample, none of whom were in severe poverty.

To sum up, among fifty-nine Stockwell households with two or more children but without an earning husband, 78 per cent were in poverty, including 47 per cent in severe poverty. In Folie-Méricourt, 23 per cent (three out of thirteen) were in poverty, all severe. Among 157 Stockwell households with an earning husband, 14 per cent were in poverty, including 1 per cent in severe poverty; in Folie-Méricourt, of 106 such households 16 per cent were in poverty, none severe.

The greater extent of poverty in the Stockwell sample was thus entirely due to its higher proportion of households without an earning husband - 27 per cent compared with 11 per cent in Folie-Méricourt. More than half of this higher proportion was due to the 'unoccupied' group, which did not exist at all in the Folie-Méricourt sample. All Folie-Méricourt households in severe poverty - there were three of them - lacked an earning husband, as did 99 per cent of such households in Stockwell.

We believe that the absence of households with an 'unoccupied' head in Folie-Méricourt, and their prominence in Stockwell, reflects an important difference in the social policies of Britain and France. In Britain an 'unoccupied' lone mother can claim supplementary benefit as of legal right, and all such mothers in the Stockwell sample were doing so. At that time (1973) no such claim could be made in France, where, apart from free medical aid and a small additional family allowance for one-parent families, the only financial assistance available was aide sociale, an ad hoc payment in emergency, linked with the idea of secours, or rescue from difficulty or danger. With no regular weekly payment to fall back on, a French lone mother had no option but to try to find work. In Britain lone mothers were receiving supplementary benefit, and most chose to manage on it, though as we have shown most were in poverty and nearly half in severe poverty, in terms of our definitions.

Our 'poverty level', as explained, included an additional 20 per cent, which most lone mothers were not getting and our use of the simplified Folie-Méricourt weightings meant that families with younger children in particular showed up as having lower incomes per equivalent adult than they would have done with supplementary benefit weights. This different result does not, of course, affect the validity of the comparisons within and between districts.

If a difference in policy explained the presence of 'unoccupied' lone mothers in Stockwell and their absence in Folie-Méricourt, it does not account for Stockwell's remaining eleven 'unoccupied' household heads who had no counterparts in Folie-Méricourt. Most of the eleven were male students or trainees. They were able to manage without paid jobs mainly because they received a student grant or training allowance, sometimes supplemented by their wife's earnings. It is not entirely clear why there were no such people in Folie-Méricourt, but part of the explanation is that students' grants were - and are - generally lower in France than Britain.

An obvious question is whether these are adequate explanations for the sharp contrast between the two samples in the presence (in Stockwell) and absence (in Folie-Méricourt) of 'unoccupied' heads of households. Might it not be instead that the Folie-Méricourt sample was in some way biased so as to exclude such people? The question is important because the

'unoccupied' make so much difference to the overall proportions
in poverty. If they were excluded from the 'all households' row
in Table III.4, the percentages in poverty would be 25 per cent
in Stockwell and 17 per cent in Folie-Méricourt, and those in
severe poverty 6 per cent and 3 per cent respectively. The
reader should bear in mind the possibility that there might have
been such a bias in the samples, in which case the contrasts
between the district in the level of income disadvantage would
be much less marked. But our investigations of the sampling
procedure in Folie-Méricourt and of such other French evidence
as we could find lead us to believe that the differences in the
samples reflected real differences.

Table III.5 relates poverty and severe poverty to the national
origin of the head of household. Table III.6 also compares
national origin groups, but in addition shows the effect on
poverty of having or not having an earning husband in the
household. The tables show that the proportion of West Indian
households in poverty was similar to that of the British households, whereas the proportion of North African households in
poverty was greater than that of the French households. Very
few West Indian households with an earning husband were in
poverty, in spite of their large families. In this they contrasted
with the North African households, whose low earnings and
large families made them the most prone to poverty of any
national origin group in either district. British-born households
were more often in poverty than French-born households. Taken
together, these comparisons show there to have been less
inequality between national origin groups in Stockwell than in
Folie-Méricourt, as already noted in Table III.3.

*Table III.5   Proportion of households in 'poverty' and 'severe poverty' by
national origin of head of household: households with two or
more children, Stockwell and Folie-Méricourt, 1973*

	Stockwell			Folie-Méricourt		
National origin of head of household	*'Poverty'* %	*'Severe poverty'* %	*Number of households in group*	*'Poverty'* %	*'Severe poverty'* %	*Number of households in group*
West Indian/ North African	25	14	65	42	11	19
Other non-British/other non-French	38	10	53	18	3	39
British/French	30	14	98	8	0	61

Table III.6   Proportion of households in 'poverty' and 'severe poverty', with and without an earning husband, by national origin of head of household: households with two or more children, Stockwell and Folie-Méricourt, 1973

	With earning husband			Without earning husband		
National origin of head of household	'Poverty' %	'Severe poverty' %	Number of households in group	'Poverty' %	'Severe poverty' %	Number of households in group
Stockwell						
West Indian	4	0	46	74	47	19
Other non-British	23	5	38	85	23	15
British	16	0	73	78	61	25
All Stockwell	14	1	157	78	47	59
Folie-Méricourt						
North African	35	0	17	100	100	2
Other non-French	18	0	34	20	20	5
French	8	0	55	0	0	6
All Folie-Méricourt	16	0	106	23	23	13

INNER CITY POVERTY: AN EVALUATION

The figures for poverty in our two study areas relate to districts which form only a small part of inner Paris and London, and an even smaller part of Britain and France. Moreover, the figures apply only to households with two or more children. The overall proportion in poverty in Stockwell in 1973 was not much higher than that in the whole of Britain at the same date: 23 per cent compared with 20 per cent (both calculated with supplementary benefit weightings rather than the simpler ones we are using). But poverty in Stockwell was highly concentrated among families with children: they accounted for 35 per cent of all those in poverty in Stockwell, compared with 13 per cent in the country generally (Shankland et al., 1977. p.56).

Why were families with children more likely to be in poverty in Stockwell than in the rest of Britain? Table III.5 suggests that this was not due to the high proportion of immigrant households in Stockwell, since national origin did not greatly affect poverty in the London district. Table III.4 shows that the occupational groups most prone to poverty were the 'unoccupied', the 'other non-manual' and the 'semi-and unskilled manual'. This last group made up 32 per cent of the Stockwell sample of households with two or more children compared to 17 per cent of all British households, and this high proportion of households headed by lower-skilled, lower-paid workers helps

to explain the relatively high figure for poverty in the sample.
In the Family Expenditure Survey Report for 1973, 4 per cent
of households are shown as having an 'unoccupied' head
(Department of Employment, 1974, p.122, Table 67), compared
to 13 per cent in the Stockwell sample and this too would help
to explain the high poverty figure in Stockwell, especially as
97 per cent of the 'unoccupied' group of households in the
sample were in poverty. The 'other non-manual' group, also
prone to poverty, was present in the same proportion (7 per
cent) in the Stockwell sample as in Britain as a whole. In suggesting that a high proportion of low-skilled and unoccupied
heads of households may explain the high proportion of households in poverty, we are of course begging the further question
of why such households should be present in such unusually
large numbers in Stockwell and other inner city areas; the
Lambeth Inner Area Study suggested that this was partly
because many such families, lacking skills and resources, would
prefer to move out but are 'trapped' in the inner city.

In seeking to compare the incidence of poverty in our Folie-
Méricourt sample with what it would have been in France as a
whole, we have no national figure for the proportion of households falling below a defined proverty line, either the one we
have been using or any other. We know, however, that the
proportion of immigrant households in Folie-Méricourt was high,
and we know furthermore from Table III.5 that in Folie-
Méricourt (unlike Stockwell) immigrant households were more
prone to poverty than the rest.Likewise, the proportion of
households with low-skilled heads was much higher in the Folie-
Méricourt sample (34 per cent) than in France as a whole (14
per cent): as in Stockwell,this group was prone to poverty.
The 'other non-manual' group, also prone to poverty, was much
the same in the Folie-Méricourt sample as in France as a whole
(14 per cent and 11 per cent respectively). It is probable,
therefore, that the proportion of households in poverty (17 per
cent) was higher than in the country generally. However, our
sample may have benefited from the Paris income differential;
we noted earlier that average household income in the Paris
region was as much as 58 per cent higher than in France as a
whole, and that the income of households with a manual worker
was 32 per cent higher.

How poverty in the Folie-Méricourt sample compared with
poverty in France as a whole then remains somewhat uncertain.
We are certain that there was more poverty in the Stockwell
sample of families with two or more children than among such
families in Britain as a whole. And we know that there was more
poverty in the Stockwell sample than in the Folie-Méricourt
sample.

How does Folie-Méricourt compare with Paris, and Stockwell
with Inner London, in the level and distribution of incomes and
in the incidence of poverty? Are they, in these respects,
typical inner areas of their respective cities? We cannot give

complete or precise answers to these questions. We can compare
the 1971 Census figures for 'economically active males' in the
Stockwell study area and the thirteen Inner London boroughs.
These show a proportion of semi-and unskilled workers (plus
a small percentage of 'unclassified' workers) as 29 per cent in
the Inner London boroughs, and 37 per cent in Stockwell. As
households headed by semi- and unskilled workers were found
to be relatively prone to poverty, this suggests that the proportion in poverty in Stockwell would be higher than in inner
London generally. But we also found the 'unoccupied' group to
be even more prone to poverty and, as the 'unoccupied' heads
of household were by definition not economically active, they
would presumably not have been enumerated among the latter,
so that the Census cannot tell us if households with 'unoccupied'
heads were especially numerous in Stockwell.

Comparing Folie-Méricourt with Paris, we know that the
French study area was chosen as one of the five Paris quartiers
with a high proportion of manual workers and a growing proportion of immigrants in the 1968 Census. Both these factors
would, as we have shown, predispose it towards poverty and,
although we cannot say precisely by how much, a higher proportion than in the rest of Paris. Almost certainly Folie-
Méricourt had more poverty in relation to the Paris average
than Stockwell had in relation to the Inner London average.
Poverty in Stockwell was somewhat above the Inner London
average, but poverty in Folie-Méricourt probably considerably
above the Paris average. As poverty in the Stockwell sample was
nearly twice as widespread as it was in the Folie-Méricourt sample, it may be inferred that, viewed as an inner city problem,
poverty loomed larger among families with children in Inner
London than in Paris.

This chapter has shown some important differences in the
patterns of incomes and of income poverty in Stockwell and
Folie-Méricourt. In summing up, we can draw the distinction
between poverty as we have measured it, using the same levels
in the two places, and income inequality or, as it might be described, 'relative poverty' by the standards of the particular
district. In these terms, the comparison shows that, among
families with children at that date, there was more income
poverty in Stockwell, more income inequality in Folie-Méricourt.

Income poverty and inequality are a large part of disadvantage but they are not the only forms, as will be seen in later
chapters. Our aim is to draw up a balance sheet of disadvantage
which goes beyond income disadvantage, or poverty in its usual
sense,important as it undoubtedly is. After dealing with disadvantages in housing, education, health and leisure, we turn,
in Chapter VI, to the theme of multiple or cumulative disadvantage. At that stage we attempt to draw up as complete a
balance sheet of comparative disadvantage as our limited data
will allow.

IV

THE INNER CITY HOUSING
PROBLEM

Inadequate housing is concentrated in the inner, older areas
of cities. This chapter looks at the incidence of two main forms
of housing disadvantage - overcrowding and lack of basic
amenities - among the households of Stockwell and Folie-
Méricourt. As with incomes, we try to place our local findings
in a national and metropolitan context. We begin by outlining
the historical origins of the housing problem, and the attempts
to solve it, in the two countries. We end by comparing the
changing pattern of housing tenures at the three geographical
levels.

ORIGINS OF THE HOUSING PROBLEM

The chronology of housing development differs in the two
countries. In France there was much building activity from 1835
to 1870, slowing down between 1871 and 1914 and even more
between the two world wars, but then rising to a high level,
especially from 1968 onwards. In England and Wales, building
activity was high in the 1870s and in most years after 1945.
During this post-war period, much of the older building was
demolished as a result of slum clearance and other kinds of redevelopment. The outcome of these differences in timing was
that by the mid-1970s there was more old housing in France
than in England and Wales, and more post-war housing in England and Wales than in France, as shown in Table IV.1.

Table IV.1   The age of the housing stock in England and Wales and France

Date of construction	England and Wales 1975 Dwellings (millions)	%	France 1973 Dwellings (millions)	%
Before 1870	1.8	10	3.5	17
1870-1944	8.3	46	9.8	48
1945 and after	7.9	44	7.0	35
Total	18.0	100	20.3	100

Sources: Department of the Environment, 1977, Pt I, Ch. 3; Seligmann, 1975.

55

In the two capital cities, the growth of population during the
nineteenth century led to a housing 'problem' which the twentieth century has not yet fully solved. In addition to some
industry, the capitals have more than their share of occupations
deriving from government, from head offices, from commerce and
from the complex of services needed to maintain so vast a population. To begin with, workers lived as near as possible to
their work. Hence, as in Folie-Méricourt, factories and dwellings proliferated side by side at high density. Stockwell had
some factories too - less than Folie-Méricourt - but most of
those who lived in the district travelled daily to work, then as
now, into Central London. In both areas, access to the centre
is still an asset, though public transport and the motor car have
long blurred the association between work and residence.

At metropolitan level, in 1974 the proportion of housing built
since the war was lower in Greater London (30 per cent) than in
England as a whole (43 per cent), with Stockwell's proportion
close to that of Greater London (28 per cent) (Central Statistical Office, 1975, p.155). The Paris agglomération, with 36 per
cent, had much the same as France as a whole, with 35 per cent,
but inner Paris had only 13 per cent and Folie-Méricourt is
unlikely to have had more. In 1962, virtually all buildings in
Folie-Méricourt pre-dated 1948, and nearly half pre-dated 1870.
By 1968 there were just seven post-war buildings, including
three residential buildings comprising forty-four dwellings.
Another difference was that, while the new housing in Stockwell
was almost entirely council housing, that in Folie-Méricourt
consisted of luxury flats, and in 1973 there was no HLM (Habit-
ation à Loyer Modéré) or other form of recently constructed
social housing in the quartier.

Few, if any, householders can afford to buy their housing by
a single payment out of income. A hundred years ago, when
average real incomes were at a far lower level, the problem for
most manual workers and their families was to find the rent the
landlord needed to provide them with shelter even at a minimum
standard. Hence the provision in Lambeth of the densely packed
two-storey housing since demolished in slum clearance schemes,
and hence the subdivision and multi-occupation of the roomier
and more solid housing.

In the 11th arrondissement of Paris, in the course of the
Haussmann reconstruction (1850-70), some workers' tenements
were built with state aid. Employers combined with the state to
provide various forms of housing for their workers, from simple
dormitories to cités ouvrières. (Maréchal and Tallard, 1973,
vol.II, p. 46). In Britain the 1875 Public Health Act and other
legislation from the 1870s onward provided for the demolition -
but not the replacement - of slum properties in the name of
health. Legally enforceable standards of construction and sanit-
ation were set at levels well above what the poorest could afford.
In 1906 the average rent plus rates of a new 'working-class'
dwelling came to about a quarter of average earnings. At the

time of the 1911 Census, between one and one and a quarter million households in Britain were sharing their housing not because of shortage - 5.6 per cent of dwellings were enumerated as vacant - but because the cost of a whole dwelling was so high in relation to average incomes (Department of the Environment, 1977, pt.I, pp. 4-5).

Real incomes increased in Britain by 0.8 per cent a year between 1880 and 1900, by 1.4 per cent a year between 1929 and 1938 and by 2.6 per cent a year between 1955 and 1975, and these accelerating increases stimulated the demand for housing. Both in Britain and France, as the countries grew richer, the possibilities of improved housing for all became greater, both because low-income households were better off in real terms and because it became politically and economically feasible for governments to tax high and average incomes and subsidize housing from the proceeds.

Even with growing state subsidies, it has taken a long time to catch up with the initial shortages. In the late 1930s, for the first time in living memory, the total number of dwellings in England and Wales was probably slightly greater than the number of households. But the Second World War brought a major set-back, and as late as 1961 dwellings remained fewer than households. By 1971 there were, in total, more dwellings than households, though there were still 430,000 more households than occupied dwellings, and 637,000 households sharing (DOE, 1977, Part I, p. 22). In France, the shortage of housing was particularly acute after the Second World War, and the effort to remedy it correspondingly great (Seligmann, 1975, pp. 19, 30).

Housing in Paris and Inner London differed from the national patterns in a number of respects. In Paris in 1970 as many as 87 per cent of dwellings dated from before 1949, compared with 63 per cent in France generally. The average Paris dwelling was small, with an area of only 47 square metres and 2.46 rooms, compared with 70 square metres and 3.57 rooms in medium-sized French towns. Only 45 per cent of Paris dwellings had both an inside WC and a bath or shower, compared with 60 per cent in the medium-sized towns. Only 22 per cent of Paris homes were owner-occupied, less than half the national proportion, and Paris rented housing also had by far the highest rents in France (Hans, 1974, pp. 47-50).

The proportion of pre-1945 housing was higher in Greater London (70 per cent in 1974) than in Britain as a whole (56 per cent) and somewhat higher than in the Paris agglomération (64 per cent in 1970). Though the number of rooms per household in Inner London (3.8 in 1971) was lower than that in England and Wales (4.7 in 1966), it was well above that in Paris (2.5 in 1970) and even slightly above that in France generally (3.6 in 1970). The proportion of owner-occupiers in Inner London was even lower in relation to the national figure than it was in Paris: 19 per cent in Inner London compared with 49 per cent in Britain in 1971.

OVERCROWDING

For historical reasons, the inner areas of London and Paris
became overcrowded and congested. Because the tide of
population turned sooner in London than in Paris, overcrowding - if not congestion - has been much reduced in Inner
London, while in some areas of Paris it is still pervasive. Paris
dwellings, as we have shown, have fewer and smaller rooms
than those in the rest of France; most of them are really only
large enough for one-and two-person households. Paris has
indeed a high proportion of such households, but families with
children remain: the Folie-Méricourt sample was made up of
them. It is therefore not surprising that many families in the
study complained of shortage of space.

Folie-Méricourt packed its substantial population on to a much
smaller area than Stockwell, itself almost entirely residential and
relatively unendowed with open spaces, large or small. The
Lambeth Inner Area Study found that some of the most stress-
ful aspects of living in Stockwell were connected with local
concentrations of high-density residential development: there,
too, households with children were the ones finding life most
difficult and making life most difficult for others. (Shankland
et al., 1977, pp.46-9). How much worse it must have been for
the Folie-Méricourt families, their space far more severely
cramped, both inside and outside the home.

To give one illustration of how their lives were affected, virtually all Folie-Méricourt immigrant households in the sample,
and three-quarters of all semi- and unskilled worker households,
referred spontaneously to problems connected with the shortage of space to sleep in. Skilled manual and 'other non-manual'
households did not seem much better off. The confined quarters
usually meant that parents had to sleep in the same room as
their children, and often in the same bed. Some children did
not sleep in their parents' apartment but in a rented room elsewhere in the building.

In one office worker's family the elder daughter, aged
twenty-one, slept in what served as dining-room, kitchen and
dressing-room; when her folding bed was opened out, people
had to step over it to get into the room. The parents and the
two sons, one of whom was sixteen, slept in the same bedroom.
There was so little space that in the morning there was a strict
rota for washing and breakfasting, the mother preferring to
stay in bed so as not to cause a 'traffic jam'. The parents said
they had to go out every evening until 11 o'clock to 'breathe'
and to leave some space for the children.

A Yugoslav family lived in a tiny concierge's lodge, the
parents sleeping in a windowless kitchen on a pull-down bed.
The two young children slept together in a folding bed in the

main room, which was used as a work room. The two older
daughters slept in a separate room on the sixth floor.

An Algerian family with three children were living in a one-
room dwelling with a small kitchen. In the room where they
slept there was a wicker cradle under the television set, a
folding mattress hooked on to the wall, and on the floor a rolled-
up mattress which was the children's bed. Two friends and
their four children were sleeping temporarily under the table
in the kitchen.

In a Tunisian Jewish family, the parents and their twelve
children were living in two rooms and a kitchen, with an
entrance-hall-cum-dining-room. The parents and the two youngest children, aged three and four, slept in a small bedroom,
while the ten other children, boys and girls aged from eight to
twenty-two, slept in the second room, two or three to a bed,
except for a three-year-old boy with poliomyelitis who had a
bed to himself.

These are extreme examples, but overcrowding was common:
87 per cent of households in the Folie-Méricourt sample lived at
more than one person to a room, and 62 per cent at more than
one-and-a-half persons. Over half of all households complained
that their dwelling was too small, this being by far the commonest complaint about their housing. People in all social categories
expressed dissatisfaction, although the cadre supérieur households had, on average, more than twice as much space as the
others.

There was more overcrowding in Stockwell than elsewhere in
London. The 1971 Census showed the following percentages
living more than one-and-a-half persons to the room: Stockwell,
6.6 per cent; Inner London, 4.8 per cent; Outer London, 1.6
per cent. Even so, the problem was much less widespread and
much less acute there than in Folie-Méricourt. Among Stockwell
households with two or more children interviewed in 1973, 51
per cent were living at more than one person to a room and 16
per cent at more than one-and-a-half persons to a room, compared with the 87 per cent and 62 per cent respectively of
Folie-Méricourt. Fewer families in Stockwell - about one in five -
complained of lack of space. As noted in Chapter I, however,
high residential density in Stockwell was linked with complaints
about the environment, both social and physical.

Stockwell has shared in a general reduction in overcrowding
in Britain. The proportion of people in private households in
England and Wales living at densities above one-and-a-half
persons to a room fell from 18.6 per cent in 1931 to 8.8 per cent
in 1951 and 2.9 per cent in 1971. Overcrowding has always been
greater in shared than in unshared dwellings, and in households
containing children than in others. The fall in overcrowding is
due to less sharing, the smaller average size of household and
the growing proportion of medium-sized homes.

Table IV.2   Overcrowding and severe overcrowding by occupation and national origin of head of household: households with two or more children, Stockwell and Folie-Méricourt, 1973

	Stockwell			Folie-Méricourt		
	Proportion of households with			Proportions of households with		
Occupation of head of household	more than one person to a room %	more than 1½ persons to a room %	No. of households in group	more than one person to a room %	more than 1½ persons to a room %	No. of households in group
Professional and managerial	50	17	19	57	19	21
Other non-manual	53	40	15	88	68	17
Skilled manual	52	11	71	98	68	40
Semi- and unskilled manual	50	13	68	93	83	41
Unoccupied	38	7	29	–	–	–
Inadequate information	50	14	14	–	–	–
National origin of head of household						
West Indian/North African	60	14	65	95	89	19
Other non-British/ other non-French	55	31	53	97	79	39
British/French	41	10	98	79	43	61
All households	51	16	216	87	62	119

Table IV.2 relates the extent of overcrowding (more than one person to a room) and of severe overcrowding (more than one-and-a-half persons to a room) in the Stockwell and Folie-Méricourt samples to the occupation and national origin of heads of household. The table shows that, at all occupational levels except professional and managerial, overcrowding and severe overcrowding in Folie-Méricourt greatly exceeded that in Stockwell. The three national origin groups in Folie-Méricourt were each likewise far more overcrowded than their counterparts in Stockwell. In Folie-Méricourt, overcrowding among the professional and managerial people, though substantial, was less than at the three other levels. In Stockwell the occupational groups were broadly alike in the degree of overcrowding. In both districts, the native-born were the least overcrowded but, whereas the North African households suffered twice as much severe overcrowding as the French households, there was no such sharp difference between the British and West Indian households, the most severely overcrowded group in Stockwell being the 'other non-British'. Thus Folie-Méricourt was not only much more overcrowded than Stockwell but also more unequal in its allocation of housing space between different kinds of people.

LACK OF HOUSING AMENITIES

Since the Second World War, in France and Britain alike, more and more households have gained access to the basic housing 'amenities' - running cold and hot water, an inside WC, a bath or shower, a separate kitchen. More homes have central heating and telephones. More families have acquired cars and domestic durables, including refrigerators, washing machines and television sets. These changes have revolutionised the standard of living of households in every social category. Though broadly similar in both countries, this general process has taken different forms, related to the different age of the housing stock, the different balance between town and country and the different proportion of public to private housing. Table IV.3 illustrates these developments and differences for three of the most basic housing amenities.

On piped water, in 1961 Britain was well ahead of France, with its larger rural population, but France had caught up by 1973. Britain was ahead also on the other two elements which in France are grouped with piped water as constituting confort - an inside WC and a bath or shower. Britain remained ahead at the end of the period, but France had greatly progressed.

Because of its high proportion of older housing, Paris, like other inner cities of France, was less well provided with basic housing amenities than urban areas of more recent construction, as many as a third of Paris dwellings being without inside WCs and baths or showers in 1973 (Hans, 1974). In Inner London, the 1971 Census figures for inside WCs and baths or showers were close to the national figures, and Stockwell was better off for these amenities, largely because of its higher than average proportion of post-war public housing.

Table IV.3   Proportion of households with three basic housing amenities: UK and France, 1961 onwards

| | Proportion of households in | | | | | |
| | United Kingdom | | | France | | |
	1961 %	1966 %	1971 %	1961 %	1966 %	1971 %
Piped water	96			78	91	97
Inside WC		72	88	40	55	70
Bath or shower	73	85	91	29	47	65
All three			88	25	43	61

Sources: for UK, Donnison, 1967, p. 54; Central Statistical Office, 1975, p. 157; DOE, 1977, Part I, pp. 27-33; for France, Seligmann, 1975, pp. 23-5.

The absence of public housing in Folie-Méricourt helps to explain its low level of amenities. In 1962, Folie-Méricourt, along with certain quartiers of the nearby 3rd and 4th arrondissements, was the worst off on this score of all the quartiers of Paris. Almost two-thirds of its dwellings had no inside WC, and only 17 per cent had a bath or shower. More than one in ten lacked running water. The 1968 Census showed a slight improvement, which apparently continued between 1968 and 1973. None the less, at the later date more than half the dwellings in the survey still had no inside WC, and four out of ten had no bath or shower, the eastern part of the quartier being markedly worse off than the western. In some enumeration districts (ilôts), especially those with a high immigrant population, the problem was acute, only 7 per cent of dwellings having an inside WC, and only 5 per cent a bath or shower. It was the western part of the quartier which had benefited most from the improvement after 1962, and the ilôts with the worst level of amenities improved less than the quartier as a whole, some having actually deteriorated.

Folie-Méricourt, and in particular its eastern side, was something of an extreme case, with levels of housing disadvantage which had been left behind by most of the rest of Paris, and even more so by most of the rest of France. The contrasts in the level of amenity enjoyed by the different occupational groups within it were also extreme. In France as a whole, national figures for 1962, 1968 and 1973 show a steady advance, by all occupational groups, in the possession of amenities; they also show greatly diminished differences between occupational groups (Seligmann, 1975, p. 28, Table 10).

In 1962 many French households, even in the better-off
groups, had lacked the elementary amenities - a quarter of the
cadres supérieurs and half the cadres moyens. This illustrates
both the relatively low level from which the French post-war
housing effort started and the distance it subsequently travelled. In Britain, the distance to be travelled, though substantial, was not so great. In 1947, for example, about half of
British households had a fixed bath; by 1969 this had risen
to more than three-quarters and by 1976 (in England) to 95 per
cent. By the end of the period, differences in domestic amenity
between occupational groups in Britain were far less than in
France, and a fixed bath had become the norm in all groups,
the proportion having one ranging only from 97 per cent at the
'top' of the occupational scale to 93 per cent among skilled and
86 per cent among unskilled manual worker households. It is
against this national contrast that the greater contrast between
the two study areas has to be viewed. In Folie-Méricourt, hardship and discomfort due to lack of household amenities was
widespread; in Stockwell, this kind of hardship was much less
common, though it could be found. Here are examples from
both areas, beginning with Folie-Méricourt.

A French petrol station attendant's family with four children
was living in two rooms on the third floor, although the mother
suffered from congenital dislocation of the hip. There were no
amenities - only a sink with cold water and some oil heaters. As
the WC was in the courtyard, they used a chemical lavatory
which they kept in the dining-room-kitchen opening on to the
stairs. The other room, whose window was kept closed because
it overlooked a factory, was used as a bedroom for the parents
and the four children.

A Tunisian Jewish family with five children had no amenities
other than a water-heater and a coal-stove with chimney pipe
running the length of the parents' bed. Both parents and
children had twice been partially asphyxiated by the stove:
they had medical certificates to prove it. The WC was two floors
down. The children were afraid to go down at night, and used
chamber pots in the kitchen.

A Yugoslav family with a seven-year-old child had no facilities of any kind, not even water, which they had to fetch from
a tap in a corridor also used by ten other families. They shared
the WC with the same families.

In Stockwell Mr and Mrs Donohue, in their thirties with two
children, had come from Northern Ireland. They had sold their
house in Belfast for £95 and now lived in just three rooms: 'The
roof leaks. The flat is riddled with mice - we had to get a cat.
There's no room for cooking, just a stove at the top of the
stairs. There's no bathroom, no hot water.'

Mrs Gordon was a wife alone with her three young children,
drawing supplementary benefit: her husband would be in prison
for the next six years. The WC was shared and there was no
bath in the house. The sink on her landing had no waste pipe;

the water simply splashed into a bucket which had to be regularly emptied down the WC.

To measure disadvantage and severe disadvantage in terms of a lack of basic housing amenities, definitions were required. The data available for Stockwell and Folie-Méricourt made it possible to define a household as having this kind of disadvantage if it lacked one out of the four following: a separate kitchen, an inside WC, running hot water and a fixed bath or shower. If it lacked three out of these four amenities, a household was counted as having a severe disadvantage. Table IV.4 shows how occupational and national origin groups in the two districts compared, on these definitions.

The table shows that the proportions with this form of disadvantage were far higher in Folie-Méricourt than in Stockwell, and that this was true for all the occupational and national origin groups except, apparently, the professional and managerial. The 'top' group in Stockwell did not have the privileged position in its housing enjoyed by this group in Folie-Méricourt. The Stockwell figures for lack of amenities by occupational group do not go in the expected direction, either for disadvantage or severe disadvantage. Also, while national origin has a very marked effect on this form of disadvantage in Folie-Méricourt, with North African households 100 per cent disadvantaged and French households 56 per cent disadvantaged - still a substantial proportion - in Stockwell 20 per cent of both British and West Indian households were disadvantaged in this way. The high proportion of West Indians living in it had had a marked levelling effect. (Compare Willmott and Aiach, 1976, pp. 171-5; Shankland et al., 1977, p. 37).

TENURE: A CHANGING PATTERN

Housing tenure is relevant to a study of housing disadvantage because some forms of tenure are more advantageous than others. As more families are able to move from a less advantageous to a more advantageous form of tenure, so the levels of housing disadvantage and of total cumulative disadvantage, fall. We end the chapter therefore by comparing the stage reached in this process of change in the two countries, inner cities and study areas, and the effects of them on housing disadvantage.

In the past, the great majority of households in both countries were the tenants of private landlords. By 1973 there had been a great increase in home ownership both in Britain and France, and an increase also, especially in Britain, in rented public or 'social' housing. The ratio between these three main tenures changed rapidly after the Second World War. The trends of change were similar in France and Britain, but the stages reached and the consequent pattern of tenure have been markedly different in the two countries. There are also

Table IV.4   Proportion with less than four and less than two basic housing amenities, by occupation and national origin of head of household: households with two or more children, Stockwell and Folie-Méricourt, 1973

	Stockwell			Folie-Méricourt		
	Proportion of households with less than four amenities %	less than two amenities %	No. of households in group	Proportion of households with less than four amenities %	less than two amenities %	No. of households in group
Occupation of head of household						
Professional and managerial	37	16	19	29	14	21
Other non-manual	33	20	15	76	18	17
Skilled manual	18	3	71	72	28	40
Semi- and unskilled manual	15	1	68	93	49	41
Unoccupied	21	3	29	–	–	–
Inadequate information	29	0	14	–	–	–
National origin of head of household						
West Indian/North African	20	5	65	100	68	19
Other non-British/ non-French	30	8	53	85	33	39
British/French	20	3	98	56	18	61
All households	23	5	216	72	31	119

differences between the tenure pattern of each capital city
and that of the rest of its country, and especially so in the
inner city areas. The patterns are compared in Table IV.5.

Table IV.5   *Proportion of households in three main housing tenures: UK and
France, Inner London and Paris, Stockwell and Folie-Méricourt;
households with two or more children, 1973*

	UK 1973 %	Inner London 1971 %	Stockwell 1973 %	France 1973 %	Paris 1970 %	Folie-Méricourt 1973 %
Home owners	52	19	19	46	22	33
Tenants in public or 'social' housing	31	30	59	11	9	0
Private tenants and others	17	51	22	43	69	67

The table shows that by 1973 home-ownership in Britain
accounted for more than half of all occupied housing. More than
half of all British households, therefore, had acquired or were
acquiring a solid capital asset - a reflection of the steady rise
over the period in real incomes and in saving. France was not
far behind. But home-ownership was by no means so strong in
Paris or Inner London.

Tenancy in public or 'social' housing grew in Britain from
just over a quarter in 1951 to just under a third in 1973, and
to about the same in Inner London. The proportion of public
tenancy was higher in the full Stockwell sample and higher
still among households with two or more children, in sharp contrast to Folie-Méricourt, without any public housing.

As home-ownership and public tenancy have grown, private
tenancy has declined. But in Paris it remained easily the pre-
dominant tenure, with 69 per cent in 1970. Among families with
two or more children in Folie-Méricourt, it was similarly pre-
dominant. It has remained much higher in Inner London than
in Britain as a whole, catering primarily for households without
children, which explains why the figure is relatively low for
the Stockwell sample of households containing children.

Privately rented housing in France includes dwellings diverse
in age, rent and legal status. The law of 1948 controls the rents
of a fair proportion of dwellings built before that date, but
there is also a stock of substandard older housing whose rent
is not controlled and a growing proportion of non-controlled,
high rented post-1948 housing, as well as quite a large component of rent-free housing. Compared to the rest of France,
Paris has a high proportion of housing rent-controlled under
the law of 1948.

At the end of 1973, the average rent over the whole of France was the equivalent of £22.22 a month (mid-1980 prices: £65.10), compared to an average rent in Britain in 1972 of £10.66 (1980: £33.04) a month for a dwelling which on average was larger and better equipped. The average rent for the Paris agglomération was the equivalent of £29.62 a month (1980: £84.12), compared to an average rent of £15.33 (1980: £47.51) a month in Greater London and the Outer Metropolitan area. Although the figure for the Paris agglomération is nearly double the Greater London figure, it would be much higher were it not for its large rent-controlled sector, and a stock of unregulated pre-1949 dwellings of poor quality, two-thirds of them lacking one or more of three basic amenities. Post-1949 dwellings, other than the relatively small amount of social housing, had an average rent of about £44 a month (1980: £125) (Durif, 1975, pp. 49-56; Central Statistical Office, 1975, p. 158, Table 12).

In 1973, at the time of the Folie-Méricourt study, the effect of the various forms of intervention by the state in the housing market was to give substantial benefit to households with around average incomes, but little or no benefit to those with low incomes (Durif and Berniard, 1971).

Comparison of the housing tenure pattern in the two countries requires a brief account of the types of household catered for by public or 'social' housing. In France, twice as many young households and half as many old households were living in HLM as in the housing stock as a whole. The average size of household in an HLM was 3.5 persons compared with an overall average of 2.9, and the average number of children was 1.4 compared with 0.8 generally, an indication of the extent to which HLM policies have favoured larger families. The average rent of HLM, not including charges for heating and other services, was less than £17.18 a month (1980: £48.79), compared with £29.29 (1980: £82.93) a month for a post-war unaided dwelling. Incomes in the middle range, or somewhat higher, predominated among HLM tenants, those with higher incomes or with lower incomes being sparsely represented. This was true also for incomes per equivalent adult. Low-income households were more likely to be found in the 36 per cent of dwellings which still lacked one or more of the basic amenities.

Although there were no HLM in Folie-Méricourt, some of its badly housed households might have applied successfully for an HLM elsewhere. The survey showed that of 72 families with five square metres or less per person or with a high index of inconfort or both, there were twenty-eight who had applied for an HLM, five who had expressed a wish for one, and a single family who expected to be housed in one on the nomination of an employer. There were 35 tenants or concierges who had apparently not applied, through scepticism or ignorance or because they found it impossible to contemplate living at such a distance from the quartier. The 72 badly housed families should almost all have had priority on the criteria then in force.

In spite of that, only thirteen had received an offer of an HLM,
all of them in the suburbs. The others had applied from nine
months to seven years earlier, without any offers being forth-
coming. The thirteen families who had been offered housing in
a suburb had declined it on two main grounds - that it was too
far away from their place of work and that they were afraid
the move would cut them off from friends and relatives and
deprive them of familiar schools, shops and community life. Of
the thirteen refusals, eight were from North African Jewish
families and three from Arab families. One family had returned
from an HLM in Bourg-la-Reine, a suburb ten kilometres to the
south of Paris, because they 'couldn't stand it'.

Building and land costs in Paris were high, and large-scale
state aid would have been needed to bring the supply of HLM
housing to the level required. In the meantime, HLM accommodation was being allocated on criteria which penalised the
poorer families, including many immigrants (Willmott and Aiach,
1976, p. 174).

Without any HLM in Folie-Méricourt there were two alterna-
tives, private renting or purchase. Over a third of the dwellings
had been found through friends or colleagues who sometimes
passed on the accommodation when they themselves left. Often
they had to pay a large sum in key money. For example, a
Tunisian 'other non-manual' worker had had to pay 8,000 Fr. -
the whole of his repatriation gratuity - for a delapidated apartment. A paint sprayer who arrived from Tunis in 1962 had to
pay 6,500 Fr. key money for one room with a tiny kitchen. A
cabinet maker, also Tunisian, paid a 9,000 Fr. deposit in 1964
for two rooms and a kitchen. A Spanish foreman paid 10,000 Fr.
in 1966 for a two-room flat with kitchen.

Stockwell, with its high proportion of local authority housing,
had a pattern of tenure different not only from that of Folie-
Méricourt, but also of Britain and even the rest of Inner London.
The proportion of home-owners was low, that of private tenants
relatively high. Most of the older housing not eliminated by slum
clearance was nineteenth-century housing originally built for
middle-class families. Some of this had been converted into self-
contained flats for rent or sale, but much of it was multi-
occupied.

Table IV.6 compares the pattern of tenures in the two districts and shows to what extent it varied in different occupational and national origin groups. The table shows that in both
areas nearly half the professional and managerial households
owned their homes, as did from a quarter to a third of the other
groups in Folie-Méricourt, while in Stockwell there were relatively few home-owners among the manual worker households.
In Stockwell most people were predominantly tenants of public
housing, as were as many as 86 per cent of the households
whose head was 'unoccupied' - another way in which social
policy was helping these families.

National origin did not make much difference to the propor-

tion of households owning their homes in either district. West
Indian and British households were the most likely to be in
public rented housing, and 'other non-British' the least likely.
West Indian households were, by a large margin, the least
likely to be in private rented housing.

Table IV.7 shows the extent to which the two forms of housing disadvantage, overcrowding and lack of amenities, varied
with housing tenure. The most striking feature of the table is
the low proportion of housing disadvantage and severe disadvantage among Stockwell public tenant households. In both
districts, home-owners suffered from housing disadvantage less
often than private tenants. The Stockwell figures show clearly
the effect of public housing in reducing levels of housing disadvantage. By providing high value for money, public housing
also helped out those in poverty or with low incomes. It was
able to do so as a result of subsidies to the housing authorities
from the exchequer and rate fund. In addition, councils gave
rent rebates on council rents to those in need, as well as rent
allowances to private tenants and rate rebates to all, whatever
their tenure. Supplementary benefit generally met all the housing costs of households receiving it.

The Lambeth Inner Area Study made systematic comparisons
of housing costs in Stockwell with those in other areas of the
London region, finding that Stockwell costs were much the same
as, or higher than, costs in areas further out. This analysis
disproved the common assumption that the concentration of
poor people in inner areas of London is a result of the avail-
ability of cheaper, older housing (Shankland et al., 1977,
p. 105; compare Willmott and Aiach, 1976, pp. 171-5).

Our comparisons have shown that France had a higher proportion of older housing than Britain, that this was especially
true of Paris, and within Paris of Folie-Méricourt. France and
Paris also had a much smaller proportion of public and 'social'
housing than Britain and London. Stockwell had a high proportion of public housing and Folie-Méricourt, none at all.

These differences led to a much higher incidence of housing
disadvantage and severe disadvantage in the Folie-Méricourt
sample than the Stockwell sample. Folie-Méricourt households
also shared a more unequal distribution of housing advantage
and disadvantage. In Folie-Méricourt, professional and managerial households had less overcrowding and much less severe
overcrowding than other households, while in Stockwell there
was no discernible difference between the occupational groups
in this respect. There was a similar contrast in the distribution
of housing amenities. National origin groups, too, shared housing advantage and disadvantage more equally in Stockwell than
in Folie-Méricourt. Whereas the North African households were
twice as likely to be severely overcrowded as the French households in the Folie-Méricourt sample, there was far less difference between the West Indian and British households in the
Stockwell sample. Similarly, whereas in Stockwell there was no

difference in lack of amenities between West Indian and British households, in Folie-Méricourt all North African households, compared to about half the French households, had less than four basic amenities.

These differences were linked with differences in housing tenure. The high proportion of Stockwell households who were tenants of public housing, and the absence of public housing in Folie-Méricourt, are the main reasons why there was less housing disadvantage and greater housing equality in Stockwell.

At the end of the last chaper, on income disadvantage, we summed up by saying that among our families with two or more children there was more income poverty in Stockwell, more income inequality in Folie-Méricourt. We can now sum up the comparison of housing disadvantage in the two areas by saying that there was more housing disadvantage in Folie-Méricourt, and also more housing inequality. The greater income disadvantage in Stockwell and the greater housing disadvantage in Folie-Méricourt, roughly balanced each other, but the inequality of incomes was reinforced in Folie-Méricourt by the inequality of its housing.

Table IV.6 Proportion of households in three housing tenures by occupation and national origin of head of household: households with two or more children, Stockwell and Folie-Méricourt, 1973

	Stockwell				Folie-Méricourt			
	Home-owners %	Public tenants %	Private tenants %	No. of households in group	Home-owners %	Public tenants %	Private tenants %	No. of households in group
Occupation of head of household								
Professional and managerial	47	32	21	19	48	0	52	21
Other non-manual	20	33	47	15	24	0	76	17
Skilled manual	7	66	27	71	33	0	67	40
Semi- and unskilled manual	16	56	28	68	29	0	71	41
Unoccupied	0	86	14	29	–	–	–	–
Inadequate information	43	43	14	14	–	–	–	–
National origin of head of household								
West Indian/North African	22	72	6	65	32	0	68	19
Other non-British/ other non-French	19	34	47	53	28	0	72	39
British/French	17	63	19	98	36	0	64	61
All households	19	59	22	216	33	0	67	119

Table IV.7   Overcrowding and lack of housing amenities by housing tenure: households with two or more children, Stockwell and Folie-Méricourt, 1973

Proportion of households with	Stockwell			Folie-Méricourt	
	Home-owners %	Tenants in public or 'social' housing %	Private tenants and others %	Home-owners %	Private tenants and others %
more than one person per room	47	46	64	78	91
more than 1½ persons per room	21	7	24	49	78
less than four amenities	29	13	42	54	80
less than two amenities	9	1	11	32	31
No. of households	34	127	55	37	82

V

EDUCATION, HEALTH AND
LEISURE

As well as the disadvantages in income, housing and environment for which comparisons have been made in earlier chapters,
there are other forms of disadvantage to explore. In this chapter we confine ourselves to those on which the two area studies
provide comparable data. Education and health are the most
obvious, if only because there has been such widespread concern about the relative disadvantages of inner city areas in
these respects. A further field in which data for the two study
areas can be compared is that of holidays and leisure. We have
not been able to include disadvantages in employment; a special
investigation was made of the local labour market as part of the
Lambeth Inner Area Study (Shankland et al., 1977, ch. 4;
also Shankland Cox Partnership/Institute of Community Studies,
1974 and 1977b), but there is unfortunately no comparable
material for Folie-Méricourt. At the time of the surveys, unemployment was relatively low in the two districts, as in Britain
and France, although it began to increase soon afterwards.

Enough information was gathered, on similar bases in the two
areas, to make comparisons possible, even though the topics
were not pursued in depth or detail. On education, the information was fuller for Folie-Méricourt than for Stockwell where,
for reasons explained later, data on the schooling of Stockwell
children were not collected; on this topic, therefore, comparison
at the local level is confined to the education received by
parents. Despite these limitations, our comparisons add to the
cumulative picture.

EDUCATIONAL DISADVANTAGE

It would have been valuable to compare the education available
for children in the two areas, and the Folie-Méricourt data
cover this in some detail, bringing out the relative disadvantage
of manual workers' children. The distribution of children between primary and secondary schools was strikingly different in
the different occupational groups. In France, unlike Britain,
this reflects educational performance, since the age at which
children move on depends on their progress in school work.
While cadre supérieur families had two children at secondary
school for every one at primary school, the ratio was reversed
in the other occupational groups, the semi- and unskilled worker
families in particular having only seven out of 75 children at

secondary school. As already suggested, this was not simply
because the children were younger; the main explanation was
retard scolaire, the process by which children are held back
with younger ones because they have not done well enough to
move up with their peers.

These and similar indications from Folie-Méricourt fit with a
large body of research on the development of the French educational system since the Second World War. There has been an
immense growth in the numbers going on to secondary and
higher education, together with absolute and relative increases
in clerical, technical and managerial occupations at the expense
of manual. But these changes have left the highest educational
levels and consequently the most prestigious and highly paid
occupations almost as inaccessible as ever to children from the
lower occupational groups - and this in spite of extensive re-
forms of the system aimed, in principle, at increasing equality
of opportunity. As this persistent failure has become more and
more apparent, disenchantment with the system has grown, and
influential marxist and quasi-marxist analysts have seen the
whole development not as a reformist vision that failed but
rather as a plot - perhaps deliberate, perhaps unconscious -
to maintain the privileged position of the higher occupational
groups and their children (see, for example, Girard et al.,
1963; Bourdieu and Passeron, 1964; Baudelot and Establet,
1971; Boudon, 1973).

In Britain, as in France, the educational system has been
expanded since the Second World War, and at the same time
there has been much study and debate on the educational disadvantage of particular groups. The report of the Plowden
Committee in 1967 and the subsequent setting up of Educational
Priority Areas were a further stimulus to research. It had at
first been intended that the Stockwell study should cover
education, but this was abandoned, not because of any failure
to recognise its importance, but because the Inner London
Education Authority (ILEA) rejected it as superfluous in view
of its own research activities (Shankland et al., 1977, p. 186).

Many studies in Britain and elsewhere have shown substantial
correlations between parents' occupational group and their
children's measured 'intelligence' (summarised in Rutter and
Madge, 1976, p. 110 ff). In the National Survey of Health and
Development, middle-class children at all ages had considerably
higher intelligence and attainment scores than the children of
manual workers. In the National Child Development Study,
parental occupation was the variable most strongly associated
with children's reading attainment at the age of seven. Other
studies have shown that mild mental retardation mainly occurs
in families where the father is a semi- or unskilled manual
worker. Mild retardation is also associated with poverty, overcrowding and a large number of children. But, though the link
with occupation and family circumstances is well established,
its exact nature and the contribution of different causal factors

have not as yet been clarified.

The ILEA literacy survey (1967) found a large gap in reading performance between immigrant and non-immigrant children beginning their second year of primary school in Inner London. In the National Foundation for Educational Research (NFER) survey of the educational provision for immigrant children, it was found that, where streaming took place, immigrants were especially concentrated in the lower divisions, and that this was most marked for children of West Indian families. There were similar disadvantages at the secondary stage. Children of West Indian families were also more likely than non-immigrant children to be placed in special schools for the educationally subnormal (Rutter and Madge, 1976, pp.270-1).

All studies which have compared home and school influences have shown that differences between schools account for far less of the variance in educational attainment than do features of the family or home. 'The Home and the School' suggested that this might be due to the type of area rather than the standard of housing (Douglas, 1964, pp. 37-8). Another study of the influence of neighbourhood on school attainment in Sunderland has obvious relevance to the issue of disadvantage in inner city areas (Robson, 1969).

Although we cannot compare the education of the children in Stockwell and Folie-Méricourt, we have comparative data on the education of the parents, in terms of the age at which it was completed, and this is set out in Table V.1.

The table shows that rather more had prolonged their education beyond the age of twenty in Folie-Méricourt than in Stockwell. More striking though is the higher proportion in Folie-Méricourt whose education had ended between the ages of seven and twelve, or who had had no education and were illiterate: there were eight illiterate heads of household in the sample. In Folie-Méricourt, therefore, there were more heads of household at the two educational extremes than in Stockwell, a further instance of its greater inequality.

The proportion with minimal education in Folie-Méricourt was much higher among North African than other non-French heads of household, and much higher in turn among other non-French than French. However, even among the French-born, 11 per cent had had minimal education, compared with none among the British-born. The differences between the national origin groups in Stockwell by no means follow the same pattern as those in Folie-Méricourt. More British-born than West Indians completed their education between the ages of thirteen and fifteen, and more West Indians than British continued their education between the ages of sixteen and nineteen. This finding is hard to interpret; it is not related to the age of the West Indian heads of household - the average age of those West Indian heads of household who had continued their education was thirty-seven, that of the British thirty-four. But, if early completion of education indicates educational disadvantage, this sample of West

Table V.1   Age of head of household at completion of education, by occupation and national origin: households with two or more children, Stockwell and Folie-Méricourt, 1973

| | Stockwell | | | | | Folie-Méricourt | | | | |
| | Age of head at end of education | | | | No. of households in group | Age of head at end of education | | | | No. of households in group |
	0-12	13-15	16-19	20+		0-12	13-15	16-19	20+	
Occupation of head of household										
Professional and managerial	0	16	58	26	19	0	24	19	57	21
Other non-manual	0	43	36	21	14	12	41	47	0	17
Skilled manual	0	83	14	3	70	33	47	19	0	36
Semi- and unskilled manual	0	79	18	0	67	47	44	3	6	36
Unoccupied	0	55	24	21	29	–	–	–	–	–
Inadequate information	0	40	60	0	10	–	–	–	–	–
National origin of head of household										
West Indian/North African	3	58	35	3	65	72	22	6	0	18
Other non-British/ other non-French	0	49	36	16	49	34	37	17	11	35
British/French	0	82	12	6	95	11	49	23	18	57
All households	1	67	24	8	209	28	41	18	13	110

Indian heads of household cannot be said to be more at a disadvantage than their British-born neighbours, unless the education they received after the age of fifteen was of a very low
standard. In contrast, in Folie-Méricourt the French-born heads
of household far surpassed the immigrants in educational attainment.

HEALTH AND DISABILITY

In both study areas, heads of household and their spouses were
asked if they, or any member of the household, were suffering
from an illness or disability which limited their activity. Table
V.2 sets out the answers.

In Folie-Méricourt there were more households with one disabled member, and many more with two disabled members, than
in Stockwell. These extra disabilities were all in the two manual
worker groups. In Stockwell there was not the same contrast
between manual and non-manual, and there were few households
with two disabled members in any group.

In Folie-Méricourt more than twice the proportion of North
African households than French households had a disabled
member, and nearly four times as many had two. The other non-
French households were in an intermediate position. In Stockwell the pattern of disability among national origin groups was
quite different: the British and West Indian households showed
more disability than the other non-British. While the presence
of the immigrant households substantially increased the rate of
disability in Folie-Méricourt, it did not do so in Stockwell.

Health and disability are matters which deserve more detailed
study than was possible in the Stockwell and Folie-Méricourt
surveys but, if these indications can be relied upon, they suggest that Stockwell had a rather high rate of disability among
parents of working age, and that this was not due to the high
proportion of immigrants. It also applied among the British-
born of all occupational groups. Folie-Méricourt had a higher
rate of disability - especially of two-members disability - and this
was concentrated among manual worker families, and among the
foreign-born rather than the French-born. Finally, more
inequality was once again evident in Folie-Méricourt than in
Stockwell.

HOLIDAYS AND LEISURE ACTIVITIES

A series of questions on leisure activities and holidays was
asked in both districts. The questions were very nearly the
same, and the results are therefore broadly if not precisely
comparable.

The question about holidays taken in the previous twelve
months was straightforward, and the results are shown in

Table V.2   Limiting illness or disability of one or more members of the household, by occupation and national origin of head of household: households with two or more children, Stockwell and Folie-Méricourt, 1973

	Stockwell			Folie-Méricourt		
	One member disabled %	Two members disabled %	No. of households in group	One member disabled %	Two members disabled %	No. of households in group
Occupation of head of household						
Professional and managerial	21	5	19	9	0	21
Other non-manual	27	0	15	29	0	17
Skilled manual	35	4	71	50	23	40
Semi- and unskilled manual	31	1	68	56	27	41
Unoccupied	34	7	29	–	–	–
Inadequate information	7	0	14	–	–	–
National origin of head of household						
West Indian/North African	31	2	65	53	37	19
Other non-British/ other non-French	17	0	53	51	18	39
British/French	38	4	98	30	10	61
All households	31	2	216	42	17	119

Table V.3. The table shows that about twice as many households in Stockwell as in Folie-Méricourt took no holiday. In
Stockwell there was little difference between occupational groups
except that a high proportion of 'unoccupied' heads of household took no holiday. In Folie-Méricourt there was a sharp difference between semi- and unskilled manual heads of household
and the rest. No doubt many of the households who took no
holiday felt that they could not afford one. That there may well
also be cultural factors is suggested by the high proportion of
West Indian and North African households taking no holiday.

Adult members of Stockwell households were asked if they
had taken part over the previous month in any out of a list of
ten leisure activities. The questions asked in Folie-Méricourt
make it possible to compare the two places on nearly all of these
activities, the only problem being a cultural one: there were no
pubs in Folie-Méricourt, while 'café' had a different meaning in
the two localities. Folie-Méricourt adults were asked if they had
been to a restaurant or café; in Stockwell they were asked both
if they had 'gone out to a restaurant for a meal in the evening'
and also 'if they had been to a pub for a drink'.

The Stockwell list of ten leisure activities comprised going to
the cinema; going to a theatre, concert or opera; going for a
drive in a car for pleasure; going out to a restaurant for a
meal in the evening; going to a pub for a drink; doing home
decorations or repairs; reading a book (not a magazine);
actually playing or taking part in sport of any kind; going to
watch a sport as a spectator (not on TV); visiting or entertain-
ing friends or relatives.

Few adults had done none of these things. Of heads of
household, only 2 per cent in Stockwell and 3 per cent in
Folie-Méricourt reported 'no leisure activity' in the preceding
month. Different members of a household often had quite different patterns of leisure activity but, ignoring this complic-
ation, the activities of one member of the household, nearly
always the head of household, are set out in Table V.4.

In Table V.5 the ten activities have been combined into four
'types'; also the average total number of activities reported by
respondents in each occupational and national origin group
has been added to provide a rough index of total leisure
activity. The table shows that the average total number of
leisure activities was appreciably higher in Folie-Méricourt
than in Stockwell, and it would be higher still if pub atten-
dance was excluded from the Stockwell total. Folie-Méricourt
comes higher on eight of the ten activities, the exceptions
being 'sport played' and 'book'. The biggest differences are
on 'cinema', 'restaurant' and 'drive'.

In both places, the 'top' occupational group had getting on
for twice as many activities as the 'bottom', with the 'unoccupied' group in Stockwell easily the lowest. West Indians
had fewer leisure activities than other non-British, and they,
in turn, fewer activities than British-born; similarly, North

Table V.3   Proportion of households where no holiday taken in previous twelve months, by occupation and national origin of head of household: households with two or more children, Stockwell and Folie-Méricourt, 1973

	Stockwell		Folie-Méricourt	
	Proportion taking no holiday %	No. of households in group	Proportion taking no holiday %	No. of households in group
Occupation of head of household				
Professional and managerial	53	19	19	21
Other non-manual	60	15	29	17
Skilled manual	56	71	18	40
Semi- and unskilled manual	54	68	49	41
Unoccupied	86	29	—	—
Inadequate information	71	14	—	—
National origin of head of household				
West Indian/North African	72	65	74	19
Other non-British/ other non-French	58	53	18	39
British/French	51	98	25	61
All households	59	216	30	119

Africans had fewer leisure activities than other non-French, who in turn had fewer than French-born. North Africans had more activities than West Indians, who apparently spent less of their leisure with friends and relatives, though more in reading books and on home repairs. Very few West Indians went to cinema, theatre or restaurant, or watched sport. The heads of household most likely to have a drink in a pub were British-born and West Indian. The variations by occupation and national origin are presumably due to a combination of economic and cultural factors.

Table V.4   Proportion of heads of household taking part in ten leisure activities in previous month: households with two or more children, Stockwell and Folie-Méricourt, 1973

	Stockwell %	Folie-Méricourt %
Cinema	9	26
Theatre, etc.	4	8
Sport played	19	10
Sport watched	8	15
Restaurant/cafe	13	45
Pub	47	–
Drive for pleasure	30	61
Book	52	43
Home repairs	35	46
Meeting friends or relatives	67	81
All households	216	119

Heads of households who took no holiday in the previous year and reported no leisure activity in the previous month other than either reading a book, doing home repairs or meeting relatives or friends may reasonably be regarded as disadvantaged in their leisure. If they had no holiday and reported no activity at all, they can be regarded as severely disadvantaged. On these criteria, the incidence of leisure disadvantage was as shown in Table V.6.

The table shows twice as much leisure disadvantage in Stockwell as in Folie-Méricourt but little severe disadvantage in either place. None were disadvantaged at the top occupational level; sizeable minorities were disadvantaged in the semi- and unskilled worker group, and in Stockwell also in the 'other non-manual' group, the most disadvantaged group in Stockwell again being the 'unoccupied'.

The West Indians were the most disadvantaged national origin group in leisure, and the French-born the least disadvantaged. The other four national origin groups all had about the same proportion disadvantaged. Leisure disadvantage is the only one

Table V.5   Types of leisure activity and total number of activities in previous month reported by heads of household, by occupation and national origin: households with two or more children, Stockwell and Folie-Méricourt, 1973

Occupation of head of household	Average number of leisure activities				Average total number of activities
	Type 1 Cinema, theatre, watching or playing sport	Type 2 Restaurant or cafe, pub, drive for pleasure	Type 3 Book, home repairs	Type 4 Meeting friends or relatives	
Professional and managerial:					
Stockwell	1.16	1.53	1.26	0.79	4.74
Folie-Méricourt	1.05	1.29	1.38	0.67	4.38
Other non-manual:					
Stockwell	0.40	1.13	1.00	0.93	3.47
Folie-Méricourt	0.53	1.06	0.82	0.59	3.00
Skilled manual:					
Stockwell	0.42	1.10	0.90	0.79	2.93
Folie-Méricourt	0.60	1.08	1.00	0.93	3.60
Semi- and unskilled manual					
Stockwell	0.34	0.79	0.71	0.74	2.51
Folie-Méricourt	0.39	0.88	0.54	0.85	2.66
Unoccupied:					
Stockwell	0.28	0.45	0.83	0.48	2.03
Inadequate information:					
Stockwell	0.13	1.00	0.88	0.88	2.88

Table V.5 (cont.)

	Average number of leisure activities				
	Type 1 Cinema, Theatre, watching or playing sport	Type 2 Restaurant or cafe, pub, drive for pleasure	Type 3 Book, home repairs	Type 4 Meeting friends or relatives	Average total number of activities
National origin of head of household					
West Indian	0.26	0.75	0.68	0.48	2.17
Other non-British	0.42	0.62	0.89	0.70	2.62
British	0.49	1.14	0.90	0.79	3.32
North African	0.42	0.84	0.32	0.79	2.37
Other non-French	0.54	0.97	0.87	0.82	3.21
French	0.69	1.20	1.08	0.82	3.79
All households:					
Stockwell	0.40	0.90	0.88	0.67	2.80
Folie-Méricourt	0.60	1.07	0.89	0.81	3.37

of the various kinds discussed in this and earlier chapters in
which the West Indians were the worst off; their relative
disadvantage was because of the high proportion who took no
holiday, the proportion with low leisure activity being roughly
the same - about a quarter - in the three Stockwell national
origin groups. Leisure disadvantage was also the only kind on
which the North African group was in a relatively favoured
position - and this in spite of the high proportion who took no
holiday.

To sum up, though the data for the two study areas were
limited to the age at which heads of household had completed
their schooling, these suggest that there was more educational
disadvantage in Folie-Méricourt, and also more educational
inequality.
    Similarly on health, there were more households with a
disabled member in Folie-Méricourt than there were in Stockwell, although the Stockwell figure was itself quite high. There
was also a substantial number of Folie-Méricourt households
with two disabled members and hardly any in Stockwell. There
was marked inequality in health disadvantage between occupational and national origin groups in Folie-Méricourt, but not
in Stockwell.
    On leisure, however, it was the Stockwell heads of house-
hold who had more disadvantage - twice as much as in Folie-
Méricourt - and there was inequality in both places between
occupational and national origin groups. This was the only form
of disadvantage investigated in which the West Indians were
the worst off and the North Africans relatively favoured.
    Having summarised the findings reported in this chapter, we
can now bring together these conclusions and those from the
two preceding chapters. We can thus draw up a rough and
ready tally of disadvantage and inequality for the samples of
families (Table V.7). There can be no doubt from this table
that Folie-Méricourt showed more inequality. It is more difficult
to be sure whether on balance it showed more disadvantage,
in view of the importance of income disadvantage, which was
greater among families in Stockwell. The least that can be said
is that the disadvantages of the Folie-Méricourt families made
their income advantage less conclusive.
    It remains our task to investigate in the next chapter the
extent to which different forms of disadvantage affected the
same households and to compare the extent of multiple disadvantage in the two study areas.

Table V.6   Proportion of heads of household disadvantaged and severely disadvantaged in respect of leisure, by occupation and national origin: households with two or more children, Stockwell and Folie-Méricourt, 1973

	Stockwell			Folie-Méricourt		
	Proportion of households			Proportion of households		
	disadvantaged %	severely disadvantaged %	No. of households in group	disadvantaged %	severely disadvantaged %	No. of households in group
Occupation of head of household						
Professional and managerial	0	0	19	0	0	21
Other non-manual	27	0	15	6	0	17
Skilled manual	16	1	71	8	0	40
Semi- and unskilled manual	21	3	68	20	7	41
Unoccupied	34	7	29	–	–	–
Inadequate information	29	0	14	–	–	–
National origin of head of household						
West Indian/North African	32	6	65	16	0	19
Other non-British/ other non-French	15	0	53	15	8	39
British/French	14	1	98	5	0	61
All households	20	2	216	10	3	119

Table V.7   Stockwell and Folie-Méricourt compared by types of disadvantage

	More disadvantage	More inequality
Income	Stockwell	Folie-Méricourt
Leisure	Stockwell	Inequality in both
Overcrowding	Folie-Méricourt	Folie-Méricourt
Lack of housing amenities	Folie-Méricourt	Folie-Méricourt
Education of parents	Folie-Méricourt	Folie-Méricourt
Health	Folie-Méricourt	Folie-Méricourt

VI

MULTIPLE DISADVANTAGE

In the last three chapters, we have looked at various disadvantages from which households can suffer. We now turn to
the question of the overlap between them: to what extent do
households suffer from these disadvantages in combination?
How far, in other words, do families in Stockwell and Folie-
Méricourt experience multiple disadvantage? And among those
with two or more children, what kinds of family do so?

Since we are again comparing the two districts, a prior question is about how far districts, as distinct from households,
differ in having concentrations of multiple disadvantage. In
answering this, we have to draw entirely on data from Britain,
since none are available from France.

DISADVANTAGES IN LOCALITIES

The concentration of different kinds of disadvantage in particular localities was examined in a government study, covering
Britain as a whole, by Holtermann (1975). The research was
based on 1971 Census data for the smallest units for which
separate figures were available, EDs (Enumeration Districts);
these contained an average of 470 people and 163 households.
Of eighteen indicators of disadvantage available in the Census
data, eleven concerned housing (including overcrowding and
lack of basic amenities) or housing tenure. There were no
direct data on income.

High levels of disadvantage were found in the inner areas
of the conurbations. Inner London, though it contained a large
number of EDs with extensive disadvantage of the kind recorded
in the Census, did not have so many of the very worst EDs
(Clydeside had the largest share of these). The degree of
spatial concentration of particular disadvantages in the EDs -
overcrowding by itself, for instance, or unemployment - was,
to quote the study, 'really quite low'. But the EDs with a high
percentage of two or more disadvantages (for example, overcrowding and unemployment) were more concentrated geographically than were EDs with separate disadvantages. Many
such EDs were in conurbations, especially Clydeside and London.
Within conurbations, inner areas had proportionately more EDs
with two or more disadvantages than other parts. However, the
pattern of spatial association between different kinds of deprivation varied, both between conurbations and within them. Nor

was it possible to generalise about the spatial distribution of
deprived EDs - sometimes they were clustered and sometimes
scattered.

Inner London proved to have many areas with fairly high
levels of multiple disadvantage (as measured in this national
study), but few with the highest levels. Figures were given
for some of the inner London boroughs, and Lambeth was shown
to have 5.3 per cent of its population in EDs highly disadvantaged in three respects: overcrowding, lack of housing amenities
and male unemployment.

This does not, of course, mean that 5.3 per cent of its
population suffered from this triple disadvantage: multiple
disadvantage in districts does not necessarily mean multiple
disadvantage in households. In order to pursue further the
question of multiple disadvantage in households, the Department
of the Environment asked the Centre for Environmental Studies
to analyse special cross-tabulations of household data drawn
from the 1971 Census for every ED in England and Wales and
every thirtieth ED in the whole of Britain. This research
included a comparison of rate of disadvantage in the area designated as the 'Lambeth Area of Need' with those in the borough
of Lambeth and in Britain as a whole. The area designated as
the Lambeth Area of Need consisted of the thirteen wards near-
est to central London, out of a total of twenty wards in the
borough. The Stockwell study area, which comprised most of
two wards and parts of three others, was included (Shaw, 1979).

Three disadvantages were considered: overcrowding, defined
as more than 1.5 persons per room; not having exclusive use
of three basic housing amenities, hot water, fixed bath and
inside WC; and having economically active males either unemployed and seeking work or unemployed and sick. The proportion of households in Britain suffering all three of these
disadvantages was 0.13 per cent. In the Lambeth Area of Need,
the proportion was 0.30 per cent, more than double the national
average. Some household types were far more prone to disadvantage than others. Amongst those most susceptible to
multiple disadvantage were households with four or more children, households in privately rented furnished accommodation,
and households with New Commonwealth-born heads.

MULTIPLE DISADVANTAGE: STOCKWELL AND FOLIE-MÉRICOURT

The earlier reports on Stockwell and Folie-Méricourt included
attempts to measure the incidence of multiple disadvantage among
the households in the survey samples, using a variety of indicators (Shankland et al., 1977, pp. 60-5; Aiach, 1975, Ch.IX).
Profiting from this experience, we have made further calculations based on households with two or more children. The
definitions of the disadvantages were adjusted so as to apply to
both sets of data and, on each of the five dimensions, a further

definition was added of a 'severe' level of disadvantage. These definitions have already been used in earlier chapters. To recapitulate, they are as follows:

Low income: weekly disposable income, net of housing costs, per equivalent adult, £8.58 or less at 1973 prices (mid-1980 prices: £24.37).
Severe: at or below £5.72 (two-thirds of £8.58) (mid-1980 prices: £16.24).
Overcrowding: more than one person per room.
Severe: more than one and a half persons per room.
Lack of housing amenities: three or less out of four amenities - indoor WC, separate kitchen, bath or shower, running hot water.
Severe: one or none of these amenities.
Poor health: a member of the household suffering from illness or disability which limits their activity.
Severe: two or more members with limiting disability.
Limited leisure: no holiday taken in previous year by head of household and no leisure activities in previous month other than reading a book, doing home repairs or meeting friends or relatives.
Severe: no holiday and no leisure activity.

Table VI.1 shows the proportion of households with two or more children in the two districts who were suffering from these five kinds of disadvantage and severe disadvantage. The proportions with low income and limited leisure were higher in Stockwell than in Folie-Méricourt, but overcrowding, lack of housing amenities and poor health were more common in Folie-Méricourt.

Table VI.1　　*Proportion of households with five kinds of disadvantage and severe disadvantage: households with two or more children, Stockwell and Folie-Méricourt, 1973*

Type of disadvantage	Disadvantaged		Severely disadvantaged	
	Stockwell %	Folie-Méricourt %	Stockwell %	Folie-Méricourt %
Low income	31	18	13	3
Overcrowding	51	87	16	62
Lack of housing amenities	24	71	5	31
Poor health	29	42	2	18
Limited leisure	21	10	2	3
Number of households	216	119	216	119

In order to analyse multiple disadvantage, we added the separate disadvantages of each household to give it a 'disadvantage score'. This is used as the basis for a set of comparisons between districts and within them. In adding up disadvantages in this way, we are of course implicitly and arbitrarily assigning the same weight to each form of disadvantage. Alternative methods of weighting were tried in an earlier analysis of the Stockwell data but the results were not radically different from those using a simply unitary index; for this reason we followed the same procedure again (Shankland Cox Partnership/Institute of Community Studies, 1977a, pp. 42-6).

Table VI.1 shows the percentage of households in the two districts which on this basis have different numbers of advantages and disadvantages. Table VI.2 shows that more of the Folie-Méricourt households were multiply disadvantaged than were those in Stockwell, largely because so many in the Paris district suffered the two housing disadvantages. If multiple disadvantage is defined as suffering from three or more of the five kinds of disadvantage, then 41 per cent of households in Folie-Méricourt and 15 per cent in Stockwell were multiply disadvantaged. The table also shows that 30 per cent of the Stockwell households had one or more severe disadvantages, as compared with 70 per cent of the Folie-Méricourt households; and that 2 per cent of the Stockwell households, but 7 per cent of those in Folie-Méricourt, were suffering from three or more severe disadvantages.

Table VI.2　Proportion of households with different numbers of disadvantages and severe disadvantages: households with two or more children, Stockwell and Folie-Méricourt, 1973

Number of disadvantages	Disadvantages		Severe disadvantages	
	Stockwell %	Folie-Méricourt %	Stockwell %	Folie-Méricourt %
0	16	8	70	30
1	37	13	23	33
2	32	39	5	30
3	9	29	2	4
4	5	10	0	3
5	1	3	0	0
Number of households	216	119	216	119

SOME DISADVANTAGED FAMILIES

Before proceeding with our analysis of suffering in the abstract, we next try to convey something of what multiple disadvantage

meant to people living in the two districts. To this end we
present examples of some of the more seriously affected households in both areas. Because we start with those whose disadvantage scores were highest the first three are Folie-
Méricourt families. All figures for incomes and rents are at 1973
prices, values at mid-1980 prices being shown in brackets.

Mr Mariquez was a Portuguese mason aged forty-five not
working because of an accident at work. He lived with his wife
and two children aged ten and seven in two rooms totalling 20
square metres, with an outside WC and no bath or running hot
water, for which the rent was £6.84 (1980: £19.43) a week.
They had taken no holiday and had no leisure activity. The main
item in their income of £13.15 (1980: £37.35) a week (£3.15(1980:
£8.95) per equivalent adult) was £11.11 (1980: £31.55) a week
earned by the wife as a nurse.

Mrs Tounzi was a Tunisian Jewish widow aged forty-nine, an
unemployed hairdresser. She suffered from nervous depression
and cervical arthrosis. She lived in two rooms, rent free as
concierge, with three of her five children; the eldest, aged
nineteen, had a blood-clot on the brain following a severe
accident, and was highly 'nervous'; the second son, aged thirteen, was also highly 'nervous' and had remained in the same
class for four years without learning anything; the third child,
aged eleven, was two years behind her age group. Mrs Tounzi's
income was £9.06 (1980: £25.73) a week (£3.35 (1980: £9.51) per
equivalent adult); she took no holiday, but had some leisure
activity (cinema, watching sport, meeting friends or relatives).

Mr Ali was a Moroccan aged forty-five, employed pressing
clothes in a steam press at a salary of £23.93 (1980: £67.96) a
week. He had a hole in his lung and had spent three years in
sanatoria. Of his three children, aged seven, four and two,
the eldest had a brain tumour, the youngest was in hospital
with diarrhoea. They lived in a single room of 18 square metres,
for which they paid £5.47 (1980: £15.53) a week, with a shared
WC in the courtyard, no kitchen, bath or running hot water.
They had not taken a holiday, but they had a car, and their
leisure activity consisted in driving in it and meeting friends
or relatives. Their income per equivalent adult was £7.81 (1980:
£22.18) a week.

Mrs Adams was a West Indian in Stockwell. Her husband was
absent, and she and her three children were living in one room
in her father's house, sharing bath, WC and kitchen; they were
without running hot water. Mrs Adams was diabetic and had
taken no holiday, but in the previous month she had gone for
a drive, read a book, watched sport and met friends. Her net
income per equivalent adult, with her husband excluded, was
£4.92 (1980: £13.97) a week.

Mrs Rogers, in Stockwell and again with no husband, was
aged forty-five and suffered from claustrophobia to an extent
that prevented her from working. With her were her married
daughter and two small children - the daughter's husband had

locked her out of her own home. The daughter too suffered
from 'nerves' and migraine and did not work. Another daughter,
aged sixteen, was unable to work because of asthma, but was
apparently receiving no benefit. A son of twenty-three and a
daughter of twenty-one were working and between them gave
their mother £15 (1980: £42.60) a week. There was also a son of
nine. These eight people were living in a four-roomed pre-war
council flat. The mother and the married daughter had taken no
holiday. The mother's only leisure activity was meeting friends;
she said the last time she had been out was at the New Year
three years previously. On the basis of the money given by the
working son and daughter to their mother, the net income of
this household was £2.02 (1980: £6.25) a week per equivalent
adult.

Mr Benamida was a Folie-Méricourt Algerian aged sixty-three,
employed as a cleaner on the Métro. He was under surveillance
by the Prefecture's Service for Dangerous Alcoholics. He lived
with his wife and seven children in one room of 42 square
metres, with outside WC and no bath or running hot water. He
had been knocked down by a car when drunk, had spent a year
in hospital and had had to change his job. The second eldest
son had been caught stealing and was under the Centre
d'éducation surveillée. Of the six children at school, three were
a year behind their age group and one two years behind. With
the help of £18.29 (1980: £51.94) a week family allowances, this
household had a net income of £10.56 (1980: £29.99) per equivalent adult. The head of the household had taken no holiday,
but his leisure activities included visiting a restaurant or café.

Mrs Medwin was a Stockwell West Indian resident aged thirty-
two who lived with her six children. They had a council flat
with five rooms but without a bath, for which she paid a rebated
rent of £3.72 (1980: £10.56). She was 'unoccupied' and the net
household income, including family allowances, appeared to work
out at only £4 (1980: £11.36) per equivalent adult. The interviewer wrote of her:

> The woman was on her own, and said she had no man -
> she's been in England 13 years and has six children
> between the ages of 12 and two. The flat, smelling of
> stale greens and dampness, is in a block that is coming
> down - out of about 120 flats, only six or seven are still
> inhabited, and the outside passages are dark and littered.
> Her two small children at home were dirty, clad in knickers
> and tops, sucking bottles, watching television (at 1 pm)
> and friendly. The woman looked old for her age. Very
> bare and seedy sitting room, with a painting of Jesus
> hanging on the wall.

Mr Mallet, London-born, was aged thirty-eight and had a
well-paid job as a BBC wireman; his son, aged eighteen, had a
job as a shoe salesman. With family allowances for the four

younger children this brought the net household income per
equivalent adult to £16.90 (1980: £48) a week. They were
council tenants in an old seven-roomed house bought for
improvement. It provided them with one room per person. There
was no hot water – the wife said 'I'm still waiting for it'. There
were difficulties with the children's schooling – they were slow
learners. The wife had a kidney ulcer and migraine which
limited her activity. The interviewer wrote of her:

> She did not seem to mind her actual accommodation, al-
> though when I interviewed her she was in the process
> of boiling water to do the washing for seven people, and
> there are a lot of repairs wanted – but she was dis-
> satisfied with the area. Throughout the interview she kept
> an anxious eye on her children playing in the street.

The Mallets had taken no holiday, and the husband had had no
leisure activities, so they were counted as severely disadvantaged in leisure, the other disadvantages being lack of running
water, and the wife's bad health.

Mr Zerga was a Folie-Méricourt Algerian, a light van driver
earning £25.64 (1980: £72.82) a week. His wife, aged thirty-one,
had seriously considered working, but the husband objected.
Both were illiterate and had never been to school. Of their
three small children, only the eldest (aged seven) was at
school, and he was a year behind his age group. The mother
had had an ovarectomy. The family lived in a single room of 17
square metres, which they owned; it had an outside WC and no
bath or running hot water. Though they had taken no holiday,
the husband had been to a restaurant or café and they had met
friends and relatives. Their net income worked out at £8.28
(1980: £23.52) per equivalent adult, just below the poverty line.

Mr Massus, French-born and in Folie-Méricourt, was employed
as a hairdresser at £17.09 (1980: £48.54) a week. He lived with
his wife and seven children in two rooms totalling 25 square
metres, with outside WC and no bath, for which he paid £1.88
(1980: £5.34) a week. Both parents left school at the age of
nine. Two of the children were behind their age group at
school – details are missing for the others. The wife suffered
from phlebitis, for which she had had an operation, and from
piles and nerves. They took no holiday; the husband went to
a café and read a book. In spite of his low pay, the £21.20
(1980: £60.21) received in family allowances lifted this household just above the poverty line.

WHO IS MULTIPLY DISADVANTAGED?

With these examples of multiple disadvantage in mind, we resume
our analysis of its incidence in the two areas. But first we must
remind the reader of the deficiencies in our data, most of which

have been mentioned in earlier chapters. There is the limitation of our samples to households with two or more children under school-leaving age. As a result of this we have failed to show the effect of the stage of life on the incidence of disadvantage, an aspect covered in the earlier reports on Stockwell (Shankland et al., 1977; Shankland Cox Partnership/Institute of Community Studies, 1974 and 1977a), and important not only in itself but also because it explains much of the difference between short-term, middle-term and long-term or irreversible disadvantage. Nor is it by any means certain that the five forms of disadvantage for which we had comparable data are an adequate selection. In particular, it is regrettable that we could not give more weight to educational, environmental and work disadvantage. Nor have we necessarily defined the five selected dimensions in the best possible way, and our choice of cut-off level has been at best pragmatic. There is also the distortion of reality which comes from the impression, likely to be given by most of our analyses, that all those below the cut-off level are equally disadvantaged and all those above it equally advantaged. In some ways it would be more helpful to measure degrees of disadvantage rather than disadvantage as an absolute condition: introducing a second cut-off level for severe disadvantage was a step in this direction.

One means of indicating plurality of disadvantage is to calculate average disadvantage scores for the two districts, and for different categories of people within them. The Folie-Méricourt sample as a whole had an average of 2.32 disadvantages per household, and the Stockwell sample 1.53. The average numbers of severe disadvantages were 1.16 and 0.39 respectively.

To evaluate the impact of disadvantage on households and to help frame policies for reducing it, it is important to know how it is distributed - whether for example it is evenly spread among all households in a district or concentrated among relatively few. It is sometimes assumed that it is highly concentrated among a minority who therefore have much more than their fair share of disadvantage. But in fact there are a whole range of possible distributions, and the distribution in a particular district or city or country can be determined only by empirical investigation. We have referred to one such investigation, commissioned by the Department of the Environment. We now look at the distribution of disadvantages in the two study areas, comparing the distribution observed with what could be expected if it was purely random. The comparisons are set out in Table VI.3.

Among families with two or more children, in Folie-Méricourt and Stockwell alike, the actual distributions were not dramatically different from what would be expected to occur by chance. In both districts, however, the proportion with four or five disadvantages was somewhat larger than expected: in Stockwell 6 per cent instead of an expected 3 per cent, in Folie-Méricourt 13 per cent instead of an expected 8 per cent. Similarly, the proportion with two or more severe disadvantages was larger

Table VI.3   'Expected' compared with 'observed' proportions with different numbers of disadvantages and severe disadvantages: households with two or more children, Stockwell and Folie-Méricourt, 1973

| | Disadvantages | | | | Severe disadvantages | | | |
| | Stockwell | | Folie-Méricourt | | Stockwell | | Folie-Méricourt | |
	'Observed' %	'Expected' %	'Observed' %	'Expected' %	'Observed' %	'Expected' %	'Observed' %	'Expected' %
0	16	14	8	2	70	67	30	20
1	37	36	13	16	23	29	33	48
2	32	33	39	42	5	4	30	27
3	9	14	29	32	2	0	4	5
4	5	3	10	7	0	0	3	0
5	1	0	3	1	0	0	0	0
Total %	100	100	100	100	100	100	100	100
Number of households	216		119		216		119	

than expected; in Stockwell 7 per cent instead of an expected
4 per cent, in Folie-Méricourt 37 per cent instead of an expected
32 per cent. Though these differences are within the ranges
that could have occurred by chance, other data suggest that
they reflect reality. As reported earlier, the special investigation for DOE found that the percentage of households in Lambeth
Area of Need with all three of the disadvantages investigated
was extremely low, but at the same time more than twice the
expected percentage (Shaw, 1979, p. 43, Table 10).

In Table VI.4, the number of disadvantages per household
is related to the occupation and national origin of household
heads. For Folie-Méricourt the table shows a clear difference
according to occupation, with the highest levels of multiple
disadvantage among the semi-skilled and unskilled, and the
lowest among the professional and managerial. It also shows a
sharp break between the professional and managerial households,
who averaged under one disadvantage per household, and the
three other occupational groups, who averaged well over two.
If the upper professional and managerial group, the cadres
supérieurs, are taken separately, they averaged 0.62 disadvantages per household, compared with an average of 1.50
for the cadres moyens. For the cadres supérieurs, severe
disadvantage was minimal, averaging 0.08 per household, compared to an average of 0.75 for the cadres moyens. Taken together, the cadres households had average numbers of disadvantages and severe disadvantages not very different from those of
their counterparts in Stockwell.

For the other occupational groups that can be compared, the
average number of disadvantages per household was higher in
Folie-Méricourt than in Stockwell. Among semi-skilled and
unskilled manual households it was nearly twice as high, while
severe disadvantage was nearly five times as high. However,
the 'unoccupied' group in Stockwell, with no corresponding
group in Folie-Méricourt, had the high average of 2.44 disadvantages including 1.11 severe disadvantages per household.
Measured in this way, these people were nearly as multiply
disadvantaged as the worst-off occupational categories in Folie-
Méricourt.

There was no clear relationship between occupation and
disadvantage in Stockwell. National origin, likewise, had little
influence there, but it had some in Folie-Méricourt, where North
African households averaged more disadvantages, and severe
disadvantages, than French. As a result of this, and whilst
French-born households had only slightly more disadvantages
than British-born, North Africans had almost twice as many as
West Indians. In fact, with an average of more than three
disadvantages per household, the North African group was, by
definition, multiply disadvantaged. And the North Africans had
nearly six times as many severe disadvantages as the West
Indians. Other non-French households also had nearly twice as
many disadvantages as other non-British households, and

Table VI.4 Average number of disadvantages and severe disadvantages, by occupation and national origin of head of household: households with two or more children, Stockwell and Folie-Méricourt, 1973

	Stockwell		Folie-Méricourt		Stockwell		Folie-Méricourt	
	Average number of disadvantages	Number in group	Average number of disadvantages	Number in group	Average number of severe disadvantages	Number in group	Average number of severe disadvantages	Number in group
Occupation of head of household								
Professional and managerial	1.17	19	0.95	21	0.39	19	0.33	21
Other non-manual	1.80	15	2.35	17	0.67	15	0.71	17
Skilled manual	1.48	71	2.53	40	0.23	71	1.20	40
Semi- and unskilled manual	1.47	68	2.80	41	0.35	68	1.73	41
Unoccupied	2.44	29	–	–	1.11	29	–	–
Inadequate information	1.00	14	–	–	0.13	14	–	–
National origin of head of household								
West Indian/North African	1.62	98	3.11	61	0.35	98	2.05	61
Other non-British/ other non-French	1.45	53	2.82	39	0.49	53	1.41	39
British/French	1.51	65	1.75	19	0.37	65	0.72	19
All households	1.53	216	2.32	119	0.39	216	1.16	119

getting on for three times as many severe disadvantages.

We also looked at the influence upon multiple disadvantage of other characteristics of households. In at least one district, four factors proved to have some relationship to households' scores on disadvantage or severe disadvantage. These were education (measured by the age at which the head of household finished his or her full-time education); housing tenure; family status (whether a single-parent or two-parent family); and the number of dependant children in the household. The various averages are shown in Table VI.5.

The table suggests the following conclusions. In Folie-Méricourt households whose heads were minimally educated had markedly higher disadvantage scores than those with more educated heads; in Stockwell their scores were only slightly higher. In both areas, private tenants had more disadvantages than home-owners, but in Stockwell, where there were many council tenants, such tenants were not as disadvantaged as private ones - not surprisingly, given the influence of council housing shown in Chapter IV. Single-parent families with four or more children were more disadvantaged than those with two or three children in Stockwell, but the difference was less marked in Folie-Méricourt.

These findings about the influence of different household characteristics upon disadvantage scores in the two places do not allow for the fact that the characteristics are themselves inter-related, that for instance West Indians in Stockwell and North Africans in Folie-Méricourt had more children, or that in both districts household heads with professional or managerial jobs were more educated and more often home-owners than those with other occupations. To try to disentangle such inter-relationships and assess the independent influence of the variables, we used multiple regression analysis.

The results of the analysis, and a description of the methods, are given in Appendix II (see Tables AII.1 and AII.2). The main point that emerged was that the variables making the largest independent difference to disadvantage scores were different in the two districts. In Folie-Méricourt, when the inter-connections between different variables were taken into account, four variables were shown to have a significant effect on a household's level of multiple disadvantage. These variables were occupation, national origin, education and housing tenure. In Stockwell, the two remaining variables - the number of children and single-parent status - were the ones which made a significant independent difference.

The regression analysis for severe disadvantage was consistent with these findings. Three of the same four variables had a significant effect in Folie-Méricourt - housing tenure dropping out - and in Stockwell only single-parent status had an effect.

A further point from the regression procedure is that it shows how much of the total variation in households' disadvantage scores is accounted for by the variables shown to have a

Table VI.5   Average number of disadvantages and severe disadvantages, by education, housing tenure, family status and number of children: households with two or more children, Stockwell and Folie-Méricourt, 1973

| | Average number of disadvantages | | | | Average number of severe disadvantages | | | |
| | Stockwell | | Folie-Méricourt | | Stockwell | | Folie-Méricourt | |
	Average number of disadvantages	Number in group	Average number of disadvantages	Number in group	Average number of severe disadvantages	Number in group	Average number of severe disadvantages	Number in group
Education of head of household								
Left school at minimum age	1.58	149	2.53	91	0.38	149	1.37	91
Left school after minimum age	1.37	67	1.50	28	0.39	67	0.46	28
Housing tenure								
Owner	1.21	34	1.97	37	0.38	34	0.98	37
Council tenant	1.49	124	–	–	0.35	124	–	–
Private tenant	1.76	55	2.43	82	0.51	55	1.27	82
Family status								
Single-parent family	1.97	32	2.00	6	0.81	32	0.83	6
Two-parent family	1.43	184	2.30	113	0.31	184	1.18	113
Number of children								
Two	1.36	115	2.20	61	0.31	115	1.03	61
Three or more	1.36	61	2.22	27	0.48	61	1.15	27
Four or more	2.53	40	2.52	31	0.35	40	1.42	31

significant effect. Their contribution was not particularly high
in Folie-Méricourt, but it was extremely low in Stockwell. Thus,
in Stockwell in particular, even the factors that did turn out to
be associated with higher disadvantage levels explained only a
little of the variation in households' scores. We come back to
this point later.

Conclusions based on such small samples must be tentative,
but it seems that occupation, education and national origin had
more effect on disadvantage in the Paris district than the
London one. This is consistent with the greater inequality we
have previously noted, and with the marked difference between
the most privileged occupational, educational and national origin
groups and the others. The fourth variable that is important
in Folie-Méricourt but not in Stockwell is housing tenure. This
does not show up as important in Stockwell, because in the
analysis council tenants, who on the whole were not very disadvantaged, were mixed with private tenants, who were. This
is an illustration of the beneficial effect of council housing,
noted in Chapter IV and also the main Lambeth report (Shankland et al., 1977).

In a district where half the households are council tenants,
the influence of housing tenure is substantial. It will be
remembered that two of our five types of disadvantage are concerned with housing. Some council tenants are overcrowded, on
our definition, but few lack the basic amenities. And since the
lower-skill occupational groups, the less educated and the
immigrants were, in 1973, proportionately or more than proportionately represented in local authority housing, the effect of
council intervention was to reduce the impact on disadvantage
scores of these other socio-economic factors as well as of tenure
itself. We would think, therefore, that this is part of the
explanation for the apparent weakness of occupation, education
and national origin as influences upon multiple disadvantage in
Stockwell.

There may be other explanations. Not only do relatively few
'professional and managerial' households elect to live in an inner
city area like Stockwell, but many of those who do seem atypical.
It will be remembered that we excluded self-employed people
and civil servants from the Stockwell sample used in this analysis, to make it comparable with the Folie-Méricourt sample.
Among those 'professional and managerial' heads of households
with two or more children who remained in the sample there
were, for example, an art teacher, a company secretary and an
advertising executive. But people like these were outnumbered
by those with less characteristic 'managerial' occupations,
including the managers of a self-service petrol station, a betting
shop and a Brixton 'boutique', two local restaurant managers
(one Cypriot, one Indian) and a Maltese 'casino inspector'.
Likewise, the household heads in the 'other non-manual' category, though they included a commercial traveller and a wages
clerk (working for a bookmaker), had more people with jobs

such as cloakroom attendant, hall porter, schoolkeeper, swimming bath attendant and toilet attendant. So far as we could
judge, the equivalent people in Folie-Méricourt - the cadres and
the employés - were by contrast not strikingly unrepresentative
of their occupational categories nationally.

Now let us put the question the other way round and ask why
the two 'family' variables - the number of children and the
number of parents - should have less impact in Folie-Méricourt
than Stockwell. The finding about family size is consistent with
what we have shown in Chapter II about the higher levels of
support, especially through family allowances, for larger families
in France than in Britain. Another cross-national study comparing a Paris district (Montreuil-sous-bois) with a London one
(Waltham Forest) drew a similar conclusion (Willmott et al., 1978
p.144).

With single-parent status the numbers are small, so particular
caution is needed, but the explanation is probably that mentioned in Chapter III. In Stockwell most of the lone parents were
unoccupied; in Folie-Méricourt, all were economically active. In
Britain, a lone mother with dependent children is legally entitled
to supplementary benefit. She can choose to stay at home, albeit
on a low income; the choice may be rather unreal since, despite
the priority given by local authorities such as Lambeth to day
nursery places for the under-fives of lone parents, she may not
be offered a place or she may, as well or instead, have dependent children over five for whom she cannot make satisfactory
arrangements.

In Folie-Méricourt, as in France generally, there is less of a
choice. No doubt partly because of the generous system of family
support and partly because there are fuller arrangements for the
day care of children at all ages, the state does not accept any
general responsibility to provide enough financial support to
allow lone mothers to stay at home. The criteria for social assistance are more stringent than in Britain and the level of support, when given, is lower.

As a result of these contrasted French and British policies,
lone mothers in Stockwell can, in comparison with those in Folie-
Méricourt, more easily keep house rather than go out of the
home to do a paid job. But their income is in consequence much
lower. They are therefore more prone to disadvantage in terms
of income and of leisure as well, and this makes them more likely
to have high scores for disadvantage and severe disadvantage
than their Parisian counterparts.

Finally there is the question of why the proportion of the
total variation in disadvantage scores accounted for by our six
household characteristics was so low. Apart from possible error
or the omission of other variables which might have been crucial,
the main explanation is one that was suggested in a discussion
of this question in the relevant Inner Area Study report:

that chance plays a large part or, to put it another way,

that people's destinies are influenced by the kinds of
factors we have been examining to a smaller extent than
might have been expected. (Shankland Cox Partnership/
Institute of Community Studies, 1977a, pp. 39-40)

We believe, therefore, that the influence of policy - as exempli-
fied by council housing in Stockwell, and family allowances in
Folie-Méricourt - can substantially reduce the impact of socio-
economic characteristics upon the circumstances of households,
rendering the level of explanation afforded by these characteristics lower than it would otherwise be.

PATTERNS OF DISADVANTAGE

We conclude this analysis of the arithmetic of multiple disadvantage in Stockwell and Folie-Méricourt by asking which combinations of disadvantages occurred most often and whether they
occurred together more often than would be expected to happen
by chance. We tried two main forms of multivariate analysis. One
was factor analysis, which had been already used in Stockwell
(Shankland Cox Partnership/Institute of Community Studies,
1977a, pp. 29-30 and pp. 69-70). In this exercise various combinations of the five disadvantages are tried, with the help of
the computer, until they fall into the groupings which 'go best'
together. The new groupings are the so-called 'factors'. Since
we were working with only five disadvantages, we asked the
computer to produce just two such groupings for each place.
The results are presented in detail in Appendix II (Tables
AII.2 and AII.3). The analysis showed, in line with the earlier
Stockwell work, that there was not a very strong tendency for
disadvantages to go together in either district. To the extent
to which they did go together, there was a difference between
the two places. In Stockwell, the two forms of housing
disadvantage fell into one grouping and the other three - low
income, poor health and limited leisure - into the second. In
Folie-Méricourt limited leisure was marked off in one 'group',
with the remaining four disadvantages going together.
The other technique adopted was cluster analysis, which was
used to group households rather than variables. With this
analysis we produced a specified number of clusters of similarly
disadvantaged households (after some experiment, we had seven
clusters in each district). Again the results are given in Appendix II (Tables AII.4 and AII.5). Again they show the housing
disadvantages going together with low income in Folie-Méricourt
but not in Stockwell. Thus both these analytical exercises confirmed that in the London district the housing disadvantages
were not strongly linked to low income, whereas in Folie-
Méricourt they were.
Since these analyses were not particularly enlightening in
other respects, we also adopted a simpler statistical approach.

This was to compare the percentage of multiply disadvantaged households suffering from each disadvantage with the percentage of all the households suffering from them. Table VI.6 sets out this comparison and shows that in Stockwell one disadvantage - disability - stood out with a high excess percentage. In Folie-Méricourt disability again had the highest excess percentage, fairly closely followed by lack of housing amenities. With due caution owing to the small numbers, this might be interpreted as indicating that disability is causally linked with other disadvantages more often than the other disadvantages. This would accord with Townsend's finding that the disabled were more likely than the non-disabled to be suffering from a wide range of other disadvantages, among them disadvantages in income, housing, leisure and employment (Townsend, 1979, pp.685-739).

It may help the policy-maker in devising a strategy for reducing disadvantage to know which disadvantages are causally linked. From the point of view of the households concerned, however, it makes little difference whether the combination of disadvantages they suffer from has arisen by chance or because of causal links. Either way, they suffer from compounded disadvantage. We have already given some examples. To understand the problems more clearly we need to know which combinations of disadvantages occur most frequently. Table VI.7 is set out in the form of a list of each of ten possible combinations of two disadvantages, nine possible combinations of three disadvantages and four possible combinations of four disadvantages, and the percentage of the Folie-Méricourt and Stockwell households who suffered from each combination.

Of possible combinations of two disadvantages in Stockwell, none stood out from the rest. In Folie-Méricourt, the most frequent combination was that of the two housing disadvantages, overcrowding and lack of amenities (39 per cent of Folie-Méricourt households). The next most frequent combinations were overcrowding plus disability and lack of amenities plus disability (both 29 per cent). Only 2 per cent of the Folie-Méricourt households combined low income and limited leisure. With three disadvantages, again no combination stood out in Stockwell. In Folie-Méricourt, one combination easily outstripped the others: overcrowding, lack of amenities and disability were combined in 29 per cent of households.

With four disadvantages, the numbers are too small for much to emerge, except that in Folie-Méricourt 9 per cent of households combined low income, overcrowding, lack of amenities and disability, and 7 per cent overcrowding, lack of amenities, disability and limited leisure. Two per cent of the sample households combined all five disadvantages.

No combination of disadvantages was outstandingly prevalent in Stockwell, but in Folie-Méricourt the commonest combinations were overcrowding and lack of amenities, overcrowding and disability, lack of amenities and disability and, among three-fold

Table VI.6   The proportion with each of five disadvantages among households with three or more disadvantages compared with the proportion with these disadvantages among all households: households with two or more children, Stockwell and Folie-Méricourt, 1973

	Stockwell						Folie-Méricourt					
	Low income %	Over-crowding %	Lack of amenities %	Disability %	Limited leisure %	No. of households %	Low income %	Over-crowding %	Lack of amenities %	Disability %	Limited leisure %	No. of households %
A Proportion with each disadvantage among households with three or more disadvantages	66	84	56	78	50	32	40	100	98	73	27	48
B Proportion with each disadvantage among all households	31	51	24	29	21	216	18	87	71	42	10	119
Excess of A over B	35	33	32	49	29		22	13	27	31	17	

Table VI.7   *Proportion of households with combinations of two, three and four out of five disadvantages: households with two or more children, Stockwell and Folie-Méricourt, 1973*

	Stockwell %	Folie-Méricourt %
Combinations of two disadvantages		
Low income and overcrowding	8	16
Low income and lack of amenities	7	15
Low income and disability	7	9
Low income and limited leisure	6	2
Overcrowding and lack of amenities	7	39
Overcrowding and disability	9	29
Overcrowding and limited leisure	6	11
Lack of amenities and disability	5	29
Lack of amenities and limited leisure	3	10
Disability and limited leisure	6	7
Combinations of three disadvantages		
Low income, overcrowding and lack of amenities	4	15
Low income, overcrowding and disability	6	9
Low income, overcrowding and limited leisure	5	3
Low income, lack of amenities and disability	2	8
Low income, lack of amenities and limited leisure	2	3
Low income, disability and limited leisure	4	3
Overcrowding, lack of amenities and disability	5	29
Overcrowding, lack of amenities and limited leisure	2	10
Lack of amenities, disability and limited leisure	1	7
Combinations of four disadvantages		
Low income, overcrowding, lack of amenities, disability	2	9
Low income, overcrowding, lack of amenities, limited leisure	1	3
Low income, overcrowding, disability, limited leisure	3	3
Overcrowding, lack of amenities, disability, limited leisure	0.5	7
Number of households	216	119

combinations, overcrowding, lack of amenities and disability.
Most of these combinations are probably due to chance, but the
figures suggest that disability in particular may be causally
linked with other disadvantages.

To sum up, our various analyses show that there was more
multiple disadvantage among the households in Folie-Méricourt
and that this was mainly because more households there suffered
from bad housing. It also seems that the mutual reinforcement
of disadvantages was weaker than has often been supposed, but
was somewhat stronger in Folie-Méricourt than Stockwell. Variations between the two places can, we believe, be largely
explained by the operation of contrasted policies, and by the
greater general inequality of French society.

VII

COMPARISONS AND POLICIES

We think it right to conclude this book by giving our own view
of what its findings imply for the framing of social policy. At
this point therefore we step outside the impartial role we have
tried to sustain in earlier chapters. The issues are large, our
data modest and our capacities limited, but unless we take this
further step the exercise will have been a hollow one.

All the forms of disadvantage we have described are, in one
way or another, the concern of social policy – of policy aimed
at increasing social welfare. Without social policies which have
led to action being taken, the extent of social and economic
disadvantage would be much greater. But social policy is by no
means the only determinant of the amount and distribution of
advantage and disadvantage in their various forms. Economic
growth or decline, demographic change, immigration, techno-
logical advance can often be at least as important. Over a given
period, changes in the distribution of disadvantage are due
partly to the implementation of policy, but partly also to the
working out of processes over which policy has little or no
control.

Obviously there has been a strong tendency in all advanced
industrial countries for the scale and scope of government
intervention to increase. Equally obviously there have been
variations in the degree of intervention and in the objectives
of social policy according to the electoral programme of the
government in power, though these effects have been limited
in practice because of economic constraints and institutional
inertia. One practical justification for comparisons such as we
have attempted in preceding chapters is that they may help to
indicate whether government interventions have had effect, and
how they might be modified so as to have more.

Social research can sometimes do this directly, with immediate
results. But experience suggests that it is likely to exert a
more gradual influence, by altering the perspectives within
which policies are conceived by politicians and interpreted by
civil servants. And it does so, to a large extent, by helping to
alter preconceptions on which previous policies of intervention
or non-intervention have been based.

It has to be emphasised that terms extensively used in social
policy discussion are seldom grounded in empirical research
but are a product of public debate. In both Britain and France,
such broadly inclusive concepts as poverty, disadvantage (or
deprivation) and inequality keep entering into contemporary

political thinking, writing and speech-making, but they are
'operationally vague' (Marshall, 1965, p.169). This operational
vagueness is compounded in more complex concepts such as
'multiple deprivation' and 'cycles of disadvantage'. Social
researchers need to make such concepts as operational as possible if they are to be measured and their incidence objectively
demonstrated. Sometimes research may show that, in a given
context, they are less quantitatively important than had often
been supposed. Some of the findings of earlier chapters tend
in this direction. But in no way do we feel that these or any of
our findings dispose of the problems of poverty, inequality and
disadvantage. The problems persist: the task is to devise better
ways of overcoming them.

POVERTY AND INEQUALITY

The effective reduction of poverty and inequality is linked to
the way in which they are measured. In presenting data on
poverty in Stockwell and Folie-Méricourt, we made use of a
measure based on the supplementary benefit scale rate plus 20
per cent (but using a simpler set of 'weights' for household
members than the supplementary benefit ones to arrive at the
income per equivalent adult). We applied this specially created
measure to income in both Britain and France.

Supplementary benefit in Britain, which has formed the basis
of many researchers' 'poverty lines' has been updated at least
once a year every year since it was instituted, as was national
assistance before it. These rates have long since ceased to have
any consistent relation to the base line from which they started,
and that base line has itself long been made obsolete by changes
in patterns of expenditure.

What we would have preferred to use for our comparative
exercise, and what would be preferable in any future comparisons by us or others, would have been an up-to-date line
based on goods, prices and patterns of expenditure current at
the time. Such a line should have the same real value one, two
or five years later. Relative poverty measures are, of course,
of some value; they can tell us something about the inequality
of incomes at the lower end of the distribution. A comparison of
expenditure patterns at mean income with those at half, a quarter or any other selected proportion of mean income can show
which goods and services households continue to purchase at
the lower income levels, and which they economise on or dis-
pense with. This information may help policy-makers to estimate
the effects of different fiscal or income maintenance policies. A
comparison of expenditure at the median level and by the poorest tenth of households provided an instructive chapter in an
important recent study (Fiegehen et al., 1977). We have ourselves made such comparisons, using Family Expenditure Survey
data, but have not included them here because they could not

be set alongside equivalent French data. But such information
is no substitute for a poverty measure with a determinate value
in real terms, representing an actual level of purchasing power.
This would be the best measure for comparisons, whether over
time or between different local or national communities.

The distinction between relative position and actual living
standards is crucial, but is seldom made in discussions about
the extent of poverty. Since the mid-1960s, the orthodox view
has been that 'poverty is a relative concept', to be measured
against average income rather than against an 'absolute' living
standard. (See, for example, Townsend, 1962; 1965; 1970; 1974;
1979; SSRC, 1968; OECD, 1976.) It has, however, generally
been admitted that relative measures of poverty - such as one
based on social benefits or a definition of households in poverty
as being all those with incomes of less than two-thirds of the
average for all households - are of little or no use for historical
comparisons (SSRC, 1968; OECD, 1976; US Department of Health,
Education and Welfare, 1976; Fiegehen et al., 1977).

The objection to using a relative measure for comparative
purposes lies in the unreal perspective of historical socio-
economic change which it provides. In their study, Fiegehen and
his colleagues concluded that 'the evidence points to neither a
significant deterioration, nor an improvement in the relative
incomes of the poor' over the period 1953-73. In that sense
'relative' poverty had neither increased nor lessened over the
period. But there had been a substantial fall in 'absolute'
poverty. When measured by a 1971 living standard held constant over time, the proportion of people in poverty thus defined
fell from about a fifth of the population in 1953 to about a
fortieth in 1973.

We recognise that the use of 'a living standard held constant
over time' requires the updating of that standard when there
have been substantial changes in goods available and in the
pattern of expenditure, but we do not envisage that such an
updating would be needed more often than perhaps once every
ten or twenty years.

One reason, perhaps, why so many socially concerned social
scientists have objected to 'absolute' measures of poverty is
that the lessening extent of poverty which they would have
usually demonstrated up to now could be used by a parsimonious
government as a pretext for not increasing, or for reducing,
social security benefits. In the early 1980s, given the priorities
of the Conservative government elected in 1979, this seems a
reasonable anxiety. But the best defence against it, we believe,
lies not in the rejection of a constant standard for measuring
poverty, but in the separation of that standard from the level
of social benefits.

Since the Second World War, successive governments in both
Britain and France have included among their declared inten-
tions the eventual elimination of poverty, at least in its absolute
or 'constant standard' sense. There can be no serious question

that poverty, in this sense, was diminishing in both France and Britain in the years preceding the Stockwell and Folie-Méricourt studies. Primarily this was the result of economic growth and of changes in the occupational structure, though these were offset by demographic changes. There were other factors such as the increasing number of working married women; in Britain the bargaining strength of trade unions and the growing effectiveness of anti-poverty pressure groups were probably influential as well. Government fiscal and income maintenance policy also played a part in ensuring that a proportion of the increasing national income was allocated to those households and people most prone to poverty. In France, social benefits were higher than in Britain and there was a statutory minimum wage which rose faster than the cost of living, but there was no national supplementary benefit system as in Britain, to act as a safety net when household incomes fell below a prescribed level.

In Britain, after 1973, although for four years real personal disposable incomes stagnated or fell back a little, the last years of the decade saw them growing again, while the proportion of the elderly continued to increase and unemployment levels remained high. What effect such recent changes have had on the incidence of poverty, in both 'absolute' and 'relative' senses, in the two countries is beyond our present scope. The French economy, on average, continued to grow faster than the British - at an average rate of 3.3 per cent a year, compared to the British 1.9 per cent. Between 1973 and 1980 the proportion of households in 'constant standard' poverty probably declined in France, and possibly in Britain.

In both countries there was a slight reduction in the inequality of incomes in the years preceding 1973 - though nothing like as large as the reduction in 'constant standard' poverty. Even more than with poverty, it is difficult to disentangle the effects of economic and demographic change from those of deliberate government intervention in bringing it about. After 1973, governments in both Britain and France expressed their intention to reduce inequality and to monitor the extent to which it was (or was not) being reduced. Thus in 1974 the terms of reference of the Royal Commission on the Distribution of Income and Wealth (the Diamond Commission) began: 'To help to secure a fairer distribution of income and wealth in the community there is a need for a thorough and comprehensive inquiry into the existing distribution of income and wealth' (RCDIW,1975). In France, one of the four commissions of inquiry set up, also in 1974, to do preparatory work for the Seventh Plan was asked 'to examine every sphere in which social inequality can be observed' (Commissariat Général du Plan, 1975). In its last report, the Diamond Commission, which was wound up by the Conservative government in 1979, reported that the slow trend towards greater equality of incomes had continued through the year 1976-77 (RCDIW, 1979). The fiscal policies of the Conserva-

tive government, and its cuts in social expenditure, halted the
trend after 1979. In France, the President and Prime Minister
continued to refer in their speeches to the reduction of social
inequalities as one of their aims; in contrast to the 1979
British budget, the French budget of that year included heavier
taxation on higher incomes and exemption for more low wage
earners.

HOUSING AND ENVIRONMENT

We have shown that there was less housing disadvantage in
Britain than in France, as a result of government intervention
over a long period. The contrast was even greater between
Stockwell, where most of the substandard housing had been
replaced, and nearly half of all households were council tenants,
and Folie-Méricourt, with no government-aided housing and
little new building of any kind. There was housing disadvantage
in Folie-Méricourt because it was untouched by government
policy in housing and physical planning. Housing was relatively
cheap, however, the households in our sample paying rents of
77 Fr. a year per square metre, compared to the Paris average
of 93 Fr. This must have been due to the high proportion of
Folie-Méricourt dwellings rent-controlled under the Law of 1948
and, to that extent, was a consequence of government intervention.
   The differences in housing and environment between Stockwell
and Folie-Méricourt were also due to differences of urban planning and inner city reconstruction policy. Since the time when
Baron Haussmann was prefect of the Seine department - and far
earlier than that - French governments have sought to make the
capital pre-eminent as a national and international centre, with
a large proportion of wealthy residents, while manual workers
and their families have been either crammed into a few residual
quartiers or dispersed into the banlieue and its grands
ensembles. This has not happened to anything like the same
extent in London, where the exodus to the outer suburbs began
much earlier, and where a policy of planned dispersal has
coincided with a powerful spontaneous outward movement, to
such effect that it has generated its own reversal in the attempt
to rehabilitate the 'inner city'. There has been relatively little
attention in France to what is regarded in Britain as the 'inner
city problem', at least until very recently.

EDUCATION, HEALTH AND LEISURE

In education, both countries have seen a vast expansion at
secondary and higher levels. It is the general verdict that
those who have taken advantage of it are predominantly from
the more privileged social groups. Neither the expansion nor

the reorganisation of the educational system has achieved the
equality of opportunity hoped for. Some critics, especially in
France, think the system has been rigged to preserve privilege
and restrict social mobility. It is doubtful if this is the whole
story. The educational motivations and expectations of parents
and children vary between occupational levels and are slow to
change. This seems to be a field in which policies come up
against a form of inertia in the system which no one yet knows
how to break down. The problems are technical as well as
political.

There was more educational inequality in Folie-Méricourt
than in Stockwell. The Paris district contained both more heads
of household who had gone on to higher education and more who
were illiterate or nearly so. West Indians were educationally no
worse off than the British-born in Stockwell, but North Africans were a great deal worse off than the French-born in Folie-
Méricourt. This might reflect differences in the countries of
origin rather than in Britain and France. A more detailed comparison of educational institutions would be needed to establish
any connection there may be between the respective educational
systems and the distributions of educational disadvantage between occupational and national origin groups in the two countries – for example, to find out whether, for the initially disadvantaged, the French institution of retard scolaire is a
greater obstacle to winning access to secondary and higher
education than equivalent British practices.

In health also more detailed comparison of institutions and
their efficacy is needed before a judgment can be passed on
the relative merits of French and British policies. Our measures
have been of limiting illness and disability in both Stockwell and
Folie-Méricourt, not of the quality of services. But they suggest some failure of policy in both countries. In health, as in
education, there seems to have been more inequality between
occupational and national origin groups in Folie-Méricourt than
in Stockwell, but we cannot say whether – or to what extent –
this was a reflection of differences in health services.

Finally, in holidays and leisure there was less disadvantage
in Folie-Méricourt than in Stockwell. As well as being related
to the higher incomes of the Folie-Méricourt families, this almost
certainly reflected the greater emphasis on paid holidays in
France, where the legal minimum in 1979 was 24 working days
a year, as a result of trade union pressures and government
concessions (Ardagh, 1977, p.409). In the choice of leisure
activities, cultural factors also come into play; this is the most
likely explanation of the West Indians appearing as the most
disadvantaged national origin group in this respect.

COMPARATIVE PERSPECTIVE

Cross-national comparison can help to suggest something about the effectiveness of alternative social policy decisions and programmes, especially when the countries concerned are as historically and geographically close, despite the differences, as are Britain and France. Each government has to decide what proportion of the national income to allot to public expenditure, and by what sort of fiscal system to raise the money; then what proportion of public expenditure should be on social security, education, health, housing and environmental services and so on. If a figure is much higher or much lower for one country than another, there is a case for asking whether it is too high or too low and, of course, how it came to be so, and whether it is practicable to change it.

The broad pattern of difference between Britain and France is well brought out in some Diamond Commission figures which confirm and supplement those which we gave in Chapter II. They are set out in Tables VII.1 and VII.2.

Table VII.1   Components of personal income as percentages of income: France, UK, 1960, 1970, 1974

	Income from employment			Income from self-employment, etc.			Income from social security, etc.		
	1960 %	*1970* %	*1974* %	*1960* %	*1970* %	*1974* %	*1960* %	*1970* %	*1974* %
France	53	55	56	31	24	22	16	21	22
UK	73	71	72	19	18	16	8	11	12

Source: Royal Commission on the Distribution of Income and Wealth, 1977, pp. 115-6, Table 53.

Table VII.2   Direct and indirect taxes and social security contributions as percentages of income: France, UK, 1960, 1970, 1974

	Direct taxes			Social security contributions			Indirect taxes			All taxes and contributions		
	1960 %	*1970* %	*1974* %	*1960* %	*1970* %	*1974* %	*1960* %	*1970* %	*1974* %	*1960* %	*1970* %	*1974* %
France	4	5	5	14	14	15	19	18	15	37	37	35
UK	10	15	15	4	5	7	16	19	15	30	39	37

Source: Royal Commission on the Distribution of Income and Wealth, 1977, pp. 119-20, Table 54.

The percentages in Table VII.1 show (as is also shown in our Table AI.2 on p.117) the greater importance of income from employment in Britain and from self-employment in France, the latter diminishing in both countries but more so in France. They also show that social security income was roughly twice as high proportionally in France as in Britain, and that it was increasing in both countries.

Table VII.2 shows that direct taxes were higher in Britain, social security contributions were higher in France and the two combined roughly the same proportion of income in both countries. Indirect taxes were also roughly the same proportionally in both countries, but were diminishing in France, the net effect being that while the total burden of taxes and contributions as a proportion of income had increased in Britain, it had slightly decreased in France. In 1974 the burden of taxation was proportionally much the same in both countries.

The French, therefore, got an increasing proportion of their income from social benefits and paid a decreasing proportion in taxes; social benefits increased in Britain too, but were a lower proportion of all income than in France, while the proportion paid in taxes increased substantially. These proportions and trends express concisely the net outcome of government intervention in both countries in terms of income.

Arguments about, for example, whether taxes are 'too high' or social security payments 'too low' are carried on within each country more or less continuously: political parties and research bodies, employers' organisations and trade unions, newspapers and pressure groups expend much time and energy on such questions. When these discussions are purely or predominantly internal, preconceptions about what is 'too high' or 'too low' tend to harden. Even if references are made to other countries, they are often casual and can be misleading outside their national context. Detailed cross-national comparison over the whole range of social policy, including trends and fluctuations, and taking into account economic and demographic factors which cannot easily be controlled or planned, is likely to be of more service to policy-makers in the longer term.

Although it may be the most important form of social disadvantage, low income is only one of a whole range of disadvantages which call for cross-national comparison, together with policies intended to reduce them. Comparison of income alone gives an unfair picture of the success achieved by governments in reducing the sum of disadvantages. To measure this, even if only approximately, some sort of index of disadvantage seems indispensable. In Chapter VI we added up the average number of disadvantages affecting households in a French and a British inner city area. As an index this is imperfect in its coverage and conjectural in its arithmetic, but it showed clearly that, although there was more poverty among families with two or more children in the British area, there was appreciably more disadvantage in the French area, and that this was predominantly housing disadvantage. The obvious inference for social policy in 1973 was that Britain should try to raise its levels of family benefit and that France should try to improve its inner city housing. Since 1973, Britain has raised levels of benefit and France has introduced new housing legislation. It is beyond our present brief to inquire how far these changes redressed the balance of social welfare between the two countries and the two areas. But it would be instructive for both governments if the comparison could be made, and we hope that it will be.

We believe that this book, for all its obvious limitations, illustrates the potential value of cross-national comparison and of the comparative perspective in the study of social policy, and suggests also that more work of the same kind could and should be done in the future. Such research can reduce confusion and deepen understanding. The overwhelming case for it is that it points the way forward to more effective solutions to those stubborn problems of inequality and disadvantage which, together with unemployment, continue to present a major challenge to the conscience and intelligence of every advanced industrial society.

APPENDIX I

Additional tables

Table A1.1 Length of time in district by occupation and national origin of heads of household: households with two or more children, Stockwell and Folie-Méricourt, 1973

| | Occupation of head of household | | | | | | | | | |
| | Professional and managerial | | Other non-manual | | Skilled manual | | Semi and unskilled manual | | Unoccupied | Inadequate information |
Number of years lived in district	Stockwell %	Folie-Méricourt %	Stockwell %	Folie-Méricourt %	Stockwell %	Folie-Méricourt %	Stockwell %	Folie-Méricourt %	Stockwell %	Stockwell %
4 or under	32	29	33	24	30	28	31	32	43	0
5-9	31	13	27	41	16	34	32	46	20	58
10-19	21	29	40	29	20	28	20	17	17	17
20 or over	16	29	0	6	34	10	17	5	20	25
Total %	100	100	100	100	100	100	100	100	100	100
Number of households	19	21	15	17	71	40	68	41	29	14

| | National origin of head of household | | | | | | All households | |
Number of years lived in district	West Indian %	Other non-British %	British %	North African %	Other non-French %	French %	Stockwell %	Folie-Méricourt %
4 or under	37	34	19	16	41	23	28	28
5-9	35	30	23	53	41	31	28	38
10-19	25	36	10	26	15	30	21	24
20 or over	3	0	48	5	3	16	23	10
Total %	100	100	100	100	100	100	100	100
Number of households	65	53	98	19	39	61	216	119

Table AI.2   Sources of household income and direct tax paid, by occupation of head of household: UK 1971, France 1970

	Self-employed		Professional and managerial		Occupation of head of household Other non-manual		Manual		Retired and unoccupied		All households	
	UK	France	UK	France	UK	France	UK	France	UK	France	UK	France
Gross household weekly income (£1 = 14.55 Fr.)	£37	£93	£51	£74	£43	£45	£40	£41	£20	£30	£38	£51
Percentage of income from:	%	%	%	%	%	%	%	%	%	%	%	%
Salaries and wages	15	11	88	77	88	71	91	68	25	15	74	45
Self-employment	69	75	1	5	8	6	1	4	1	19	7	27
Investment, etc.	12	6	9	2	8	2	3	1	33	8	10	4
Social benefit	4	8	2	16	4	21	5	27	41	58	9	24
Total	100	100	100	100	100	100	100	100	100	100	100	100
Percentage of gross income paid in direct tax	16	9	17	7	16	10	16	8	8	6	16	9

To convert to mid-1980 prices, multiply 1970 figures by 3.636, 1971 figures by 3.324.
Sources: for UK, Department of Employment, 1972, p. 85, Table 34; for France, Roze, 1974, p. 32.

*Table AI.3   Net income of households with different categories of
self-employed heads, France 1970*

Occupation of head of household	No. of households (thousands)		Per cent of all households %		Net household income per week (a)	
Industrial employers	81		0.5		£243	
Self-employed professionals	113	340	0.7	2.1%	198	£187
Commercial employers	146		0.9		147	
Shopkeepers	648		4.0		64	
Artisans	470	242	2.9	13.2%	61	£ 52
Farmers	1024		6.3		41	

(a) £1 = 14.55 Fr.
Sources: Bandérier, 1973, p. 16, Table 1; Roze, 1974, Table A.

Table AI.4   *Household income per week and its sources, by occupation of
head of household: households with two or more children,
husband earning, Stockwell and Folie-Méricourt, 1973*

Occupation of head of household	Stockwell		Folie-Méricourt	
Professional and managerial	£	%	£	%
Husband's earnings	58.53	79	81.40 (a)	77
Wife's earnings	10.60	14	9.28	9
Other earnings	1.93	3	6.96	7
Social benefits	3.00	4	9.06	8
Total income	74.06	100	106.64	100
No. of households in group	15		14	
Other non-manual	£	%	£	%
Husband's earnings	31.45	71	27.30	59
Wife's earnings	9.41	21	8.32	18
Other earnings	1.35	3	1.93	4
Social benefits	1.80	4	9.06	19
Total income	44.01	100	46.61	100
No. of households in group	10		15	
Skilled manual	£	%	£	%
Husband's earnings	42.70	69	37.06	73
Wife's earnings	9.86	16	3.59	7
Other earnings	7.40	12	2.55	5
Social benefits	2.07	3	7.40	15
Total income	62.03	100	50.61	100
No. of households in group	53		38	
Semi-skilled and unskilled manual	£	%	£	%
Husband's earnings	34.17	64	25.49	64
Wife's earnings	7.80	16	2.92	7
Other earnings	5.17	11	3.71	9
Social benefits	2.17	4	8.12	20
Total income	49.21	100	40.24	100
No. of households in group	47		36	

(a) £1 = 13.50 Fr.

Table AI.5   Household income per week and its sources, by national origin of head of household: households with two or more children, husband earning, Stockwell and Folie-Méricourt, 1973

National origin of head of household	Stockwell		Folie-Méricourt	
West Indian/North African	£	%	£	%
Husband's earnings	34.47	61	25.50 [a]	58
Wife's earnings	15.76	28	2.21	5
Other earnings	3.79	7	4.43	10
Social benefits	2.34	4	12.12	27
Total income	56.36	100	44.26	100
No. of households in group	36		17	
Other non-British/ other non-French	£	%	£	%
Husband's earnings	35.48	73	30.07	70
Wife's earnings	4.44	9	3.16	7
Other earnings	7.13	15	2.65	6
Social benefits	1.37	3	7.11	17
Total income	48.47	100	42.99	100
No. of households in group	28		33	
British/French	£	%	£	%
Husband's earnings	43.56	74	46.21	73
Wife's earnings	7.37	12	6.68	11
Other earnings	5.74	10	3.18	5
Social benefits	2.50	4	7.23	11
Total income	59.17	100	63.30	100
No. of households in group	61		53	
All households	£	%	£	%
Husband's earnings	39.13	70	37.62	70
Wife's earnings	9.15	16	4.82	9
Other earnings	5.49	10	3.47	6
Social benefits	2.20	4	8.00	15
Total income	55.97	100	53.91	100
No. of households in group	125		103	

(a) £1 = 13.50 Fr.

Table AI.6   *Proportion of wives working and contributions to household income per working wife, by occupation and national origin of head of household: households with two or more children, husbands earning, Stockwell and Folie-Méricourt, 1973*

	Proportion of wives working	No. of households in group	Contribution per working wife
Occupation of head of household			
Professional and managerial	%		£
Stockwell	60	15	17.66 [a]
Folie-Méricourt	21	14	43.16
Other non-manual			
Stockwell	60	10	15.68
Folie-Méricourt	27	15	24.95
Skilled manual			
Stockwell	51	53	17.12
Folie-Méricourt	29	38	12.41
Semi- and unskilled manual			
Stockwell	45	47	15.18
Folie-Méricourt	33	36	10.63
National origin of head of household			
West Indian	89	36	17.24
North African	6	17	(37.61) [b]
Other non-British	29	28	15.70
Other non-French	41	33	11.21
British	46	61	15.63
French	30	53	19.72
All households			
Stockwell	54	125	16.40
Folie-Méricourt	29	103	16.73

(a) £1 = 13.50 Fr.
(b) A single case: the French wife of a Tunisian husband

APPENDIX II

Analyses of multiple disadvantage

In seeking to analyse the relationship between multiple disadvantage and the characteristics of households we used multiple regression. In trying to disentangle the inter-relationships
between the disadvantages we used factor analysis and cluster
analysis. The analyses are explained and results presented for
each of these in turn.

MULTIPLE REGRESSION

One of our main interests in Chapter VI was to understand the
influence of various factors upon multiple disadvantage. We
have presented some of the results in the form of tabulations,
but there are limits to what can be learned from such tabulations, partly because the numbers in particular cells may be
small and partly because the different factors are usually
correlated with each other. The purpose of multiple regression
is to allow one to look simultaneously at the contributions made
to the 'dependent variable' - in this case a multiple disadvantage score - by several different household variables.

We wanted to determine the influence of household factors -
the independent variables - upon the deprivation scores (and
severe deprivation scores) of households. The 'household variables', as we have described them, were expressed in binary
form. In terms of each variable, in other words, households
were separated into two categories, for example those in which
the head of household had finished his or her education at or
below the minimum education age and those whose education had
continued beyond that age. We did this because there are
powerful technical arguments, with variables of the kind that
we were using, for expressing them in this binary form (Johnston, 1963). The exception was the number of children, where
the variable was expressed in terms of a number ranging from
two to eight.

The household variables used in the analysis have already
been described in Chapter VI (pp.96-9). In deciding on the
components of the multiple disadvantage score we had been
guided by the data available on a comparable basis for the two
districts; in deciding on the 'cut-off' points for the different
disadvantages, we had used a series of preliminary analyses
to suggest the most sensible levels that could be used across the
two countries. Similarly in deciding upon the household vari-

ables to use, we were guided by a series of preliminary analyses, as reported in Chapter VI. We excluded those variables that, in preliminary multiple regression analyses, proved to either add little by way of explanation or to be correlated too highly with others. In a somewhat similar fashion as that used to determine the 'cut-off' points for disadvantage, we carried out a series of exercises to test out the effects of dividing households up in different ways. The final six variables, and the definitions used, are shown in Chapter VI.

The results were carried out in a step-wise fashion. This method first selects the independent variable which accounts for most of the variance in the dependent variable, and then successively adds in others in order of significance, in other words according to their contribution to variation in the dependent variable (see Dixon, 1968). If any independent variable does not have a statistically significant influence on the dependent variable – the disadvantage score or severe disadvantage score – it is not included in the equation.

*Table AII.1   Contribution of household variables to households'
disadvantage scores*

Stockwell

Mean deprivation score without influence of variables shown:		Household variable	Difference made by variable	F
	0.62			
		Number of children	+0.29	22.67
$r^2 = 0.13$		Single-parent family	+0.52	7.52
$F = 15.15$				

Folie-Méricourt

Mean deprivation score without influence of variables shown:				
	0.95			
		North African origin	+0.79	19.88
$r^2 = 0.38$		Minimum education	+0.68	18.96
$F = 17.21$		Low-skill occupation	+0.19	6.40
		Tenant	+0.18	4.30

The results of the regressions are given in Tables AII.1 and AII.2. As well as listing the variables which had a statistically significant influence on the scores, and showing the contribution that each made on average, the table gives their 'F' value. This indicates the statistical significance of the contribution made by the particular variable, and depends on the consistency of the relationship between the disadvantage score and the particular household variable (the 'goodness of fit' in statistical terminology), rather than the size of the contribution. The r^2 value shows the proportion of variance in the score (disadvantage or severe disadvantage) accounted for by the independent variable shown. Where r^2 is shown as 0.13, as for Stockwell in Table AII.1, this means that 13 per cent of the variance is explained by the dependent variables shown. The F value shown below the r^2 value is a measure of the statistical significance of the contributions taken together.

Table AII.2   Contribution of household variables to households' severe disadvantage scores

Stockwell				
Mean deprivation score without influence of variables shown:	0.31	Household variable	Difference made by variable	F
		Single-parent family	+0.50	16.34
$r^2 = 0.07$				
$F = 16.34$				
Folie-Méricourt				
Mean deprivation score without influence of variables shown:	0.20			
$r^2 = 0.35$		North African origin	+0.65	17.21
$F = 21.06$		Minimum education	+0.61	11.25
		Low-skill occupation	+0.50	8.86

FACTOR ANALYSIS

The question we wanted to answer was whether there were any distinctive 'clusters' of disadvantages. Which of them, if any, tended to go together? We have in Chapter VI presented some material showing the correlations between disadvantages. We have also shown the proportions of households in the two districts suffering from different combinations of three or more disadvantages. As we have reported, there did not seem a particularly strong tendency for the various disadvantages to cluster into marked groupings.

But we wanted to explore this further, and it was for this

that we carried out factor analysis. So few households suffered severe disadvantages that it did not seem worthwhile to carry out this analysis for them. The results of the factor analysis are given in Table AII.3. The object of this exercise was to use the computer to create new 'factors', in effect the kinds of cluster of variables we were seeking. Because we were dealing with only five disadvantages, it seemed sensible to limit the 'factors' or clusters to two. The figures opposite each variable show the correlation between that variable and each of the newly created two factors. A minus sign means that the particular variable is negatively correlated with the new factor. For each variable the highest of its correlations with the two new factors is 'boxed'. Thus those factors which are 'boxed' are those which tend to cluster together.

Table AII.3   Factor analysis of disadvantages included in multiple disadvantage score

	Correlation of variables with two factors	
Stockwell	*Factor 1*	*Factor 2*
Low income	−0.178	0.116
Overcrowding	0.119	0.026
Lack of housing amenities	0.730	−0.115
Poor health	0.064	0.425
Limited leisure	0.019	0.233
Folie-Méricourt		
Low income	0.165	0.011
Overcrowding	0.384	−0.012
Lack of housing amenities	0.372	0.163
Poor health	0.092	0.088
Limited leisure	−0.021	0.462

'Boxed' variables are those which show the highest correlation with the newly created 'factors'.

CLUSTER ANALYSIS

We wanted to identify the main types of household according to the conditions of disadvantage from which they suffered. Many households suffered few or none. But what of the households that were disadvantaged? Was there a sizeable minority suffering only in terms of housing? What disadvantages were characteristic of the households? Did sizeable numbers suffer a condition of health and leisure problems, for example? To try to answer such questions, we needed to develop a special

classification of households in Stockwell and another of households in Folie-Méricourt.

Using cluster analysis, we grouped the households in each
sample into seven types according to their scores across the
range of five disadvantages. The choice of the number of types
was, as always, a matter of compromise. A large number of
types gives greater detail but is relatively complicated; with
fewer types, detail is sacrificed for the sake of simplicity.
Even when all of the 148 households in the Stockwell sample
were grouped into as few as seven types, it proved possible
to preserve 69 per cent of the original variability. In other
words, the variance between the seven types amounted to 69
per cent of that between the original 148 households; the remaining 31 per cent of the original variance occurred within
types and was therefore lost. In Folie-Méricourt, seven types
captured 81 per cent of the total variance, with only 19 per
cent lost in classification. This difference confirms again that
it was easier to 'explain' multiple disadvantage in the French
district.

Table AII.4, based on the Stockwell sample, shows the scores
of seven household types on the five disadvantages. The household types can be described as follows:

Type 1   Households suffering an income disadvantage
         (16.7 per cent of total)
Type 2   Households suffering no particular disadvantage
         (27.9 per cent)
Type 3   Households suffering a health disadvantage
         (17.2 per cent)
Type 4   Households suffering housing disadvantage
         (14.0 per cent)
Type 5   Households suffering housing and health
         disadvantages (5.6 per cent)
Type 6   Households suffering multiple disadvantages
         - especially non-housing disadvantages
         (7.9 per cent)
Type 7   Households suffering leisure disadvantage
         (10.7 per cent)

Table AII.5, for Folie-Méricourt, again shows the scores of
seven household types on the five clustering variables. The
household types defined by cluster analysis can be described
thus:

Type A   Households suffering a health disadvantage
         and some overcrowding (7.6 per cent of all
         households)
Type B   Households suffering health and housing
         disadvantages (18.5 per cent)
Type C   Households suffering housing disadvantages
         (26.9 per cent)

Type D   Households suffering income and some housing
         and health disadvantages (14.3 per cent)
Type E   Households suffering intense leisure
         deprivation and multiple other disadvantages
         (10.1 per cent)
Type F   Households suffering no particular disadvantage
         (17.6 per cent)
Type G   Households suffering some health and amenity
         disadvantages (5.0 per cent)

The results of the two analyses confirm our earlier conclusions in two important respects. First, Stockwell contained a
higher proportion of households suffering no particular disadvantage (27.9 per cent compared with 17.6 per cent in Folie-
Méricourt) and proportionately fewer households suffering
multiple disadvantages of various kinds. Second, housing
disadvantages show up as more distinct from other forms of
disadvantage in Stockwell than in Folie-Méricourt. Only two of
Stockwell's types suffer significant levels of housing disadvantages and other problems (types 5 and 6) compared with five
in Folie-Méricourt (types A, B, D, E and G). Furthermore,
even Stockwell's type 6 (households suffering multiple disadvantages) reveals a distinct bias towards non-housing disadvantages. Scores on the housing variables are low, and the
low positive score on the housing amenity variable probably
indicates the effect of local authority housing. By contrast,
Folie-Méricourt's type E (households suffering intense leisure
disadvantage and multiple other disadvantages) includes fairly
high positive scores on the housing variables.

Table AII.4   Standardised scores of the seven household types in Stockwell

	Type 1	Type 2	Type 3	Type 4	Type 5	Type 6	Type 7
Overcrowding	−0.181	−0.114	−0.149	0.386	0.486	0.398	−0.231
Lack of housing amenities	−0.403	−0.536	−0.536	1.865	1.865	0.029	−0.536
Low income	1.503	−0.666	−0.080	−0.521	−0.124	1.247	−0.666
Poor health	−0.666	−0.666	1.503	−0.666	1.503	0.992	−0.288
Limited leisure	−0.500	−0.500	−0.500	−0.417	−0.083	2.000	2.000

To facilitate comparison, the scores on all five disadvantages are presented in standard
deviations about a zero mean. Hence a value of 2.000 indicates a score which is two standard
deviations above the mean, and a value of −2.000 indicates a score which is two standard
deviations below the mean.

Though itself a simplification, the cluster analysis emphasises
that the patterns of multiple disadvantage are by no means as
simple as might be supposed. Housing and income disadvantages
may be more distinct in Stockwell than in Folie-Méricourt, but
Stockwell's type 6 has above-average scores on both. Again

although housing and income disadvantages are more closely
related in Folie-Méricourt than in Stockwell, both areas contain
some households living in poor housing but without major
income disadvantages (types 4 and C). By revealing something
of the patterns of association between the disadvantages, the
cluster analyses therefore illustrate something of the complexity
of patterns of multiple disadvantage.

*Table AII.5   Standardised scores of the seven household types
in Folie-Méricourt*

	Type A	Type B	Type C	Type D	Type E	Type F	Type G
Overcrowding	0.380	0.380	0.380	0.380	0.0380	−0.911	−2.633
Lack of housing amenities	−1.614	0.619	0.619	0.357	0.619	−1.614	0.247
Low income	−0.449	−0.449	−0.449	2.225	0.219	−0.449	−0.449
Poor health	1.175	1.175	−0.851	0.102	0.331	−0.851	0.449
Limited leisure	−0.335	−0.335	−0.335	−0.335	2.986	−0.335	−0.335

To facilitate comparison, the scores on all five disadvantages are presented in standard
deviations about a zero mean. Hence a value of 2.000 indicates a score which is two standard
deviations above the mean, and a value of −2.000 indicates a score which is two standard
deviations below the mean.

REFERENCES

Aiach, P. (1975), 'Vivre à Folie-Méricourt: Étude des processus cumulatifs
d'inégalités', Institut National de la Santé et de la Recherche Médicale,
Le Vesinet.
Ardagh, J. (1977), 'The New France', 3rd edn, Penguin, Harmondsworth.
Bandérier, G. (1973), Les revenus fiscaux des ménages en 1970 et leur
évolution depuis 1962, 'Économie et Statistique', 52, INSEE, Paris.
Baudelot, C. and Establet, R. (1971), 'L'école capitaliste en France', Maspéro,
Paris.
Boudon, R. (1973), 'L'Inégalité des chances', A. Colin, Paris.
Bourdieu, P. and Passeron, J.-C. (1964), 'Les Héritiers', Minuit, Paris.
Central Statistical Office (1975), 'Social Trends', No. 6, HMSO, London.
Commissariat Général du Plan (1975), 'Rapport de la Commission des
Inégalités sociales', La Documentation Française Paris.
Deakin, N. and Ungerson, C. (1977), 'Leaving London: Planned Mobility and
the Inner City', Heinemann, London.
Department of Employment (1963), 'Family Expenditure Survey, 1962', HMSO,
London.
Department of Employment (1971), 'Family Expenditure Survey, 1970', HMSO,
London.
Department of Employment (1972), 'Family Expenditure Survey, 1971', HMSO,
London.
Department of Employment (1974), 'Family Expenditure Survey, 1973', HMSO,
London.
Department of the Environment (1977), 'Housing Policy Technical Volume',
HMSO, London.
Dixon, W.J. (ed.) (1968), 'Biomedical Computer Programs', University of
California Press, Berkeley and Los Angeles.
Donnison, D.V. (1967), 'The Government of Housing', Penguin,
Harmondsworth.
Douglas, J.W.B. (1964), 'The Home and the School', MacGibbon & Kee, London.
Durif, P. (1975), Les loyers en novembre 1973, 'Économie et Statistique',
65, INSEE, Paris.
Durif, P. (1976), Les Français, voient-ils 'objectivement' leur logement?,
'Économie et Statistique', 74, INSEE, Paris.
Durif, P. and Berniard, S. (1971), De quelques inégalités entre locataires,
'Économie et Statistique', 25, INSEE, Paris.
Fiegehen, G.C., Lansley, P.S. and Smith, A.D. (1977), 'Poverty and Pro-
gress in Britain 1953-73', Cambridge University Press.
Girard, A., Bastide, J. and Pourcher, G. (1963), Enquête nationale sur
l'entrée en sixième et la démocratisation de l'enseignement, 'Population', 18.
Hans, M.E. (1974), Les conditions de logement au centre des agglomérations,
'Économie et Statistique', 55, INSEE, Paris.
Hibbert, J. (1975), International comparisons on the basis of purchasing
power parities, 'Economic Trends', 265, HMSO, London.
Holtermann, S. (1975), Areas of urban deprivation in Great Britain: an
analysis of 1971 Census data, 'Social Trends', No.6, HMSO, London.
Institut National de la Statistique et des Études Économiques (1977), 'Code
des Catégories socio-professionnelles', Paris.
Johnston, J. (1963), 'Econometric Methods', McGraw-Hill, New York.

Maréchal, P. and Tallard, M. (1973), 'Les Causes socio-économiques des mauvais logements', Centre de Recherches et de Documentation sur la Consommation, Paris.

Marshall, T.H. (1965), 'Social Policy in the Twentieth Century', Hutchinson, London.

Murie, A. (1974), 'Household Movement and Housing Choice', Occasional Paper No. 28, Centre for Urban and Regional Studies, University of Birmingham.

Office of Population Censuses and Surveys (1971), 'Classification of Occupations, 1970', HMSO, London.

Office of Population Censuses and Surveys (1973), 'The General Household Survey', HMSO, London.

Organisation for Economic Cooperation and Development (1976), 'Public Expenditure on Income Maintenance Programmes', Paris.

Pay Board (1974), 'Advisory Report on London Weighting', HMSO, London.

Picard, H. (1972), Situation relative des prix de détail dans les agglomérations de plus de 20,000 habitants, en octobre, 1971, 'Économie et Statistique', 37, INSEE, Paris.

Robson, B.T. (1969), 'Urban Analysis', Cambridge University Press.

Rossi, P.H. (1955), 'Why Families Move', Free Press, Chicago.

Royal Commission on Local Government in England (1969), 'Community Attitudes Survey', Research Report No. 9, HMSO, London.

Royal Commission on the Distribution of Income and Wealth (1975), 'Report No. 1, Initial Report on the Standing Reference', HMSO, London.

Royal Commission on the Distribution of Income and Wealth (1977), 'Report No. 5, Third Report on the Standing Reference', HMSO, London.

Royal Commission on the Distribution of Income and Wealth (1979), 'Report No. 7, Fourth Report on the Standing Reference', HMSO, London.

Roze, H. (1974), Impôts directs et transferts sociaux: effet sur l'échelle des revenus de 1962 a 1970, 'Économie et Statistique', 59, INSEE, Paris.

Rutter, M. and Madge, N. (1976), 'Cycles of Disadvantage', Heinemann, London.

Seligmann, N. (1975), Le parc de logements en 1973 et leur évolution depuis dix ans, 'Économie et Statistique', 64, INSEE, Paris.

Shankland Cox and Associates (1968), 'Expansion of Ipswich', HMSO, London.

Shankland Cox Partnership/Institute of Community Studies (1974), 'Project Report' (IAS/LA/1), Department of the Environment.

Shankland Cox Partnership/Institute of Community Studies (1975a), 'Labour Market Study' (IAS/LA/4), Department of the Environment.

Shankland Cox Partnership/Institute of Community Studies (1975b), 'People, Housing and District' (IAS/LA/5), Department of the Environment.

Shankland Cox Partnership/Institute of Community Studies (1975c), 'Poverty and Multiple Deprivation', (IAS/LA/10), Department of the Environment.

Shankland Cox Partnership/Institute of Community Studies (1977a), 'Second Report on Multiple Deprivation' (IAS/LA/15), Department of the Environment.

Shankland Cox Partnership/Institute of Community Studies (1977b), 'Local Employers Study' (IAS/LA/16), Department of the Environment.

Shankland, G., Willmott, P. and Jordan, D. (1977), 'Inner London: Policies for Dispersal and Balance', Final Report of the Lambeth Inner Area Study, HMSO, London.

Shaw, M. (1979), 'Multiple Deprivation in Lambeth Inner Area of Need', Working Note 552, Centre for Environmental Studies, London.

Social Science Research Council (1968), 'Research on Poverty', Heinemann, London.

Szulc, N. (1966), 'Aspects de l'insalubrité et étude des problèmes posés par la rénovation dans le XIe arrondissement', Mémoire DES, Institut de Géographie, Paris.

Townsend, P. (1962), The meaning of poverty, 'British Journal of Sociology'. 13,3.

Townsend, P. (ed.) (1970), 'The Concept of Poverty', Heinemann, London.

Townsend, P. (1974), Poverty as relative deprivation: resources and style of living, in Wedderburn, D. (ed.), 'Poverty, Inequality and Class Structure', Cambridge University Press.
Townsend, P. (1979), 'Poverty in the United Kingdom', Allen Lane, London.
Townsend, P. and Abel-Smith, B. (1965), 'The Poor and the Poorest', Occasional Papers on Social Administration No. 17, G.Bell, London.
United States Department of Health, Education and Welfare (1976), 'The Measure of Poverty', Technical Paper III, A review of the definition and measurement of poverty. vol.1; Summary Review Paper.
Willmott, P. and Aiach, P. (1976), Deprivation in Paris and London, in Willmott, P. (ed.), 'Sharing Inflation? Poverty Report, 1976'. Temple Smith, London.
Willmott, P., Willmott, P.M. and McDowell, L. (1978), 'Poverty and Social Policy In Europe: a Pilot Study in the United Kingdom, Germany and France', Institute of Community Studies, London.
Willmott, P. and Young, M. (1960), 'Family and Class in a London Suburb', Routledge & Kegan Paul, London.
Wilson, H. and Womersley, L. (1969), 'Expansion of Northampton', HMSO, London.
Young, M. (1970), A new voice for the neighbourhood, 'What?' Winter, 1970.
Young, M. and Willmott, P. (1957), 'Family and Kinship in East London', Routledge & Kegan Paul, London.
Young, M. and Willmott, P. (1973), 'The Symmetrical Family: A Study of Work and Leisure in the London Region', Routledge & Kegan Paul, London.

INDEX

Aiach, P., 1, 5
Algerians, 13, 14
Arabs, 13, 14, 68
Avenue de la République, 13

Bethnal Green, 20
Birmingham, 2
Boulevard de Belleville, 13, 14, 15
Boulevard de la République, 25
Boulevard Voltaire, 13
Brixton, 14, 15

Caisse d'Allocations Familiales, 5
Catégories socio-professionnelles (CSPs), 6
Census data, 3, 11, 12, 22, 33, 54, 57, 59, 62, 87, 88
Central London, 56
Centre for Environmental Studies, 88
Child benefits, 3, 115
Cluster analysis, 102, 125-8
Clydeside, 87
Commissariat Général du Plan, 1, 110
Community, 20
Council estates, 4, 15
Council housing, 56, 68, 98, 100
Crime, 17, 19, 22, 37, 38, 43

Department of the Environment (DOE), 15, 88, 94, 96
Deprivation, 8, 107; multiple, 9, 108
Disability, 77, 103
Disadvantage, 9, 37, 54, 75, 84, 107; cycles of, 108; multiple, 37, 54, 84, 87-106, 122-8
Durand Gardens, 14

Education, 54, 73-7, 84, 98, 100, 111
Educational Priority Areas, 74
Electric Avenue, 15
Employment, 73
Enumeration Districts (EDs), 87, 88
Environment, 11-26, 111; physical, 17, 22; social, 17, 19, 22
Environmental disadvantage, 25, 26; likes and dislikes, 15-18, 26

Factor analysis, 102, 124-5
Family allowances, 3, 46, 50, 101

Family Expenditure Survey, 3, 53, 108
Fiegehen, G.C., 109
Folie-Méricourt, 1, 4, 18, 25; past and present, 11-14; sample, 4, 5 and passim

General Household Survey, 3
Greater London, 3, 20, 33, 35, 56, 57, 67
Greater London Council, 4

Habitations à loyer modéré (HLM), 12, 56, 67, 68
Haussmann, Baron, 11, 13, 56, 111
Health, 54, 77, 84, 112
Hibbert, J., 28
Holidays, 73, 77-86, 112
Holtermann, S., 87
Home ownership, 64, 66, 68, 69
Household incomes, 27-36, 37-54, 101
Housing, 54, 55-72, 111; amenities, lack of, 55, 61-4, 69, 70, 88, 100, 103; costs, 46, 48, 69; estates, 14, 15; tenure, 64-70, 98, 100

Immigrants, 7, 13, 17, 19, 21, 52, 53, 58, 62, 68, 75, 77, 100
Inequality, 31, 32, 35, 37-54, 70, 77, 84, 106, 107, 108-11, 112
Inner London, 3, 4, 11, 17, 21, 33, 35, 52, 54, 57, 58, 59, 66, 68, 69, 87
Inner London Education Authority (ILEA), 74; literacy survey, 75
Institut National de la Santé et de la Recherche Médicale (INSERM), 1
Institute of Community Studies, 2, 20

Jews, 13, 14, 68

Lambeth, Borough of, 1, 2, 88; Council, 4
Lambeth Area of Need, 88, 96
Lambeth Inner Area Study, 2, 4, 9, 15, 48, 53, 58, 69, 73, 101
Landor Road, 15
Lansdowne Gardens, 14
Larkhall, 14

Leisure, 54, 77-86, 101, 112
Liverpool, 2
London, 1, 11, 14, 33, 35, 111
London County Council, 4
London Metropolitan Region, 20
London Weighting, 35
Lone mothers, 7, 49, 101

Madge, C., 2
Madge, N., 9
Montreuil-sous-bois, 101
Multiple regression analysis, 98, 122-4
Multivariate analysis, 102

National Child Development Study, 74
National Foundation for Educational Research (NFER), 75
National origin groups, 7, 45 and passim
National Survey of Health and Development, 74
Neighbourhood, 20, 21, 41, 43
North Africans, 7, 15, 17, 18, 19, 21, 23, 45, 46, 51, 61, 64, 68, 69, 75, 79, 81, 84, 96, 98, 112

'Oases', 4, 14, 15, 25
Occupational classification, 6; structure, 7, 27, 33, 110 and passim
One-parent families, 8, 50, 98, 101
Outer London, 59
Outer Metropolitan Area, 67
Overcrowding, 9, 23, 55, 58-61, 69, 88, 100

Paris, 1, 5, 11, 33, 35, 52, 53, 56, 57, 58, 61, 62, 66, 68, 69, 111; agglomération, 3, 15, 33, 35, 56, 57, 67; 11th arrondissement, 1, 11, 12, 13, 56; region, 35
Pay Board, 35
Philadelphia, 22, 25
Place de la République, 11, 14
Plowden Committee, 74
Poverty (low income), 8, 32, 35, 37-54, 70, 107, 108-11, 112
Privately rented housing, 66, 68
Public housing, 66, 67, 68, 69, 70
Purchasing power parities, 28, 48

Rate rebates, 69
Rent rebates, 69
Rents, 67, 69, 111
Residence, length of, 20
Residential mobility, 22, 23
Retail price index, 29
Retard scolaire, 74, 112
Rossi, P., 22, 25
Royal Commission on the Distribution of Income and Wealth (RCDIW, also known as the Diamond Commission), 110, 113
Rutter, M., 9

Salaire minimum interprofessionel de croissance (SMIC), 32, 35
Shankland Cox Partnership, 2
Shankland, G., 2
Social and Community Planning Research, 15
Social policies, 50, 101, 102, 103, 106, 107-15
Social Science Research Council, 2
Socio-economic Groups (SEGs), 6
Stockwell, 1, 2, 4, 20, 21, 22, 25; past and present, 14-15; sample, 5, 15 and passim
Stockwell Park, 14
Supplementary benefit, 32, 35, 50, 52, 69, 101, 108, 110
Supplementary Benefits Commission, 48

Townsend, P., 103
Tunisians, 13, 14

Unemployment, 49, 73, 88
Unoccupied heads of household, 7, 35, 48, 49, 50, 52, 53, 54, 68, 79, 96

Vandalism, 4, 17, 19, 22

Walker, P., 2
Waltham Forest, 101
West Indians, 8, 15, 17, 21, 22, 23, 45, 46, 51, 61, 64, 69, 70, 75, 79, 81, 84, 96, 98, 112
Willmott, P., 1
Working wives, 44, 45, 110

Routledge Social Science Series

Routledge & Kegan Paul   London, Henley and Boston

39 Store Street,
London WC1E 7DD
Broadway House,
Newtown Road,
Henley-on-Thames,
Oxon RG9 1EN
9 Park Street,
Boston, Mass. 02108

Contents

International Library of Sociology 2
General Sociology 2
Foreign Classics of Sociology 2
Social Structure 3
Sociology and Politics 3
Criminology 4
Social Psychology 4
Sociology of the Family 5
Social Services 5
Sociology of Education 5
Sociology of Culture 6
Sociology of Religion 6
Sociology of Art and Literature 6
Sociology of Knowledge 6
Urban Sociology 7
Rural Sociology 7
*Sociology of Industry and
Distribution* 7
Anthropology 8
Sociology and Philosophy 8
International Library of
Anthropology 9
International Library of Phenomen-
ology and Moral Sciences 9
International Library of Social
Policy 9
International Library of Welfare and
Philosophy 10
Library of Social Work 10
Primary Socialization, Language and
Education 12
Reports of the Institute of
Community Studies 12
Reports of the Institute for Social
Studies in Medical Care 13
Medicine, Illness and Society 13
Monographs in Social Theory 13
Routledge Social Science Journals 13
Social and Psychological Aspects of
Medical Practice 14

*Authors wishing to submit manuscripts for any series
in this catalogue should send them to the Social Science Editor,
Routledge & Kegan Paul Ltd, 39 Store Street,
London WC1E 7DD.*
● *Books so marked are available in paperback.*
○ *Books so marked are available in paperback only.*
*All books are in metric Demy 8vo format (216 × 138mm approx.)
unless otherwise stated.*

International Library of Sociology
General Editor   John Rex

GENERAL SOCIOLOGY

Barnsley, J. H. The Social Reality of Ethics. *464 pp.*
Brown, Robert. Explanation in Social Science. *208 pp.*
● Rules and Laws in Sociology. *192 pp.*
Bruford, W. H. Chekhov and His Russia. *A Sociological Study. 244 pp.*
Burton, F. and **Carlen, P.** Official Discourse. *On Discourse Analysis, Government Publications, Ideology. About 140 pp.*
Cain, Maureen E. Society and the Policeman's Role. *326 pp.*
● **Fletcher, Colin.** Beneath the Surface. *An Account of Three Styles of Sociological Research. 221 pp.*
Gibson, Quentin. The Logic of Social Enquiry. *240 pp.*
Glassner, B. Essential Interactionism. *208 pp.*
Glucksmann, M. Structuralist Analysis in Contemporary Social Thought. *212 pp.*
Gurvitch, Georges. Sociology of Law. *Foreword by Roscoe Pound. 264 pp.*
Hinkle, R. Founding Theory of American Sociology 1881–1913. *About 350 pp.*
Homans, George C. Sentiments and Activities. *336 pp.*
Johnson, Harry M. Sociology: *A Systematic Introduction. Foreword by Robert K. Merton. 710 pp.*
● **Keat, Russell** and **Urry, John.** Social Theory as Science. *278 pp.*
Mannheim, Karl. Essays on Sociology and Social Psychology. *Edited by Paul Keckskemeti. With Editorial Note by Adolph Lowe. 344 pp.*
Martindale, Don. The Nature and Types of Sociological Theory. *292 pp.*
● **Maus, Heinz.** A Short History of Sociology. *234 pp.*
Myrdal, Gunnar. Value in Social Theory: *A Collection of Essays on Methodology. Edited by Paul Streeten. 332 pp.*
Ogburn, William F. and **Nimkoff, Meyer F.** A Handbook of Sociology. *Preface by Karl Mannheim. 656 pp. 46 figures. 35 tables.*
Parsons, Talcott and **Smelser, Neil J.** Economy and Society: *A Study in the Integration of Economic and Social Theory. 362 pp.*
Payne, G., Dingwall, R., Payne, J. and **Carter, M.** Sociology and Social Research. *About 250 pp.*
Podgórecki, A. Practical Social Sciences. *About 200 pp.*
Podgórecki, A. and **Łos, M.** Multidimensional Sociology. *268 pp.*
Raffel, S. Matters of Fact. *A Sociological Inquiry. 152 pp.*
● **Rex, John.** Key Problems of Sociological Theory. *220 pp.*
Sociology and the Demystification of the Modern World. *282 pp.*
● **Rex, John.** (Ed.) Approaches to Sociology. *Contributions by Peter Abell, Frank Bechhofer, Basil Bernstein, Ronald Fletcher, David Frisby, Miriam Glucksmann, Peter Lassman, Herminio Martins, John Rex, Roland Robertson, John Westergaard and Jock Young. 302 pp.*
Rigby, A. Alternative Realities. *352 pp.*
Roche, M. Phenomenology, Language and the Social Sciences. *374 pp.*
Sahay, A. Sociological Analysis. *220 pp.*
Strasser, Hermann. The Normative Structure of Sociology. *Conservative and Emancipatory Themes in Social Thought. About 340 pp.*
Strong, P. Ceremonial Order of the Clinic. *267 pp.*
Urry, John. Reference Groups and the Theory of Revolution. *244 pp.*
Weinberg, E. Development of Sociology in the Soviet Union. *173 pp.*

FOREIGN CLASSICS OF SOCIOLOGY

● **Gerth, H. H.** and **Mills, C. Wright.** From Max Weber: *Essays in Sociology. 502 pp.*

● **Tönnies, Ferdinand.** Community and Association *(Gemeinschaft und Gesell-schaft).\Translated and Supplemented by Charles P. Loomis. Foreword by Pitirim A. Sorokin. 334 pp.*

SOCIAL STRUCTURE

Andreski, Stanislav. Military Organization and Society. *Foreword by Professor A. R. Radcliffe-Brown. 226 pp. 1 folder.*

Broom, L., Lancaster Jones, F., McDonnell, P. and **Williams, T.** The Inheritance of Inequality. *About 180 pp.*

Carlton, Eric. Ideology and Social Order. *Foreword by Professor Philip Abrahams. About 320 pp.*

Clegg, S. and **Dunkerley, D.** Organization, Class and Control. *614 pp.*

Coontz, Sydney H. Population Theories and the Economic Interpretation. *202 pp.*

Coser, Lewis. The Functions of Social Conflict. *204 pp.*

Crook, I. and **D.** The First Years of the Yangyi Commune. *304 pp., illustrated.*

Dickie-Clark, H. F. Marginal Situation: *A Sociological Study of a Coloured Group. 240 pp. 11 tables.*

Giner, S. and **Archer, M. S.** (Eds) Contemporary Europe: *Social Structures and Cultural Patterns, 336 pp.*

● **Glaser, Barney** and **Strauss, Anselm L.** Status Passage: *A Formal Theory. 212 pp.*

Glass, D. V. (Ed.) Social Mobility in Britain. *Contributions by J. Berent, T. Bottomore, R. C. Chambers, J. Floud, D. V. Glass, J. R. Hall, H. T. Himmelweit, R. K. Kelsall, F. M. Martin, C. A. Moser, R. Mukherjee and W. Ziegel. 420 pp.*

Kelsall, R. K. Higher Civil Servants in Britain: *From 1870 to the Present Day. 268 pp. 31 tables.*

● **Lawton, Denis.** Social Class, Language and Education. *192 pp.*

McLeish, John. The Theory of Social Change: *Four Views Considered. 128 pp.*

● **Marsh, David C.** The Changing Social Structure of England and Wales, 1871–1961. *Revised edition. 288 pp.*

Menzies, Ken. Talcott Parsons and the Social Image of Man. *About 208 pp.*

● **Mouzelis, Nicos.** Organization and Bureaucracy. *An Analysis of Modern Theories. 240 pp.*

● **Ossowski, Stanislaw.** Class Structure in the Social Consciousness. *210 pp.*

● **Podgórecki, Adam.** Law and Society. *302 pp.*

Renner, Karl. Institutions of Private Law and Their Social Functions. *Edited, with an Introduction and Notes, by O. Kahn-Freud. Translated by Agnes Schwarzschild. 316 pp.*

Rex, J. and **Tomlinson, S.** Colonial Immigrants in a British City. *A Class Analysis. 368 pp.*

Smooha, S. Israel: Pluralism and Conflict. *472 pp.*

Wesolowski, W. Class, Strata and Power. *Trans. and with Introduction by G. Kolankiewicz. 160 pp.*

Zureik, E. Palestinians in Israel. *A Study in Internal Colonialism. 264 pp.*

SOCIOLOGY AND POLITICS

Acton, T. A. Gypsy Politics and Social Change. *316 pp.*

Burton, F. Politics of Legitimacy. *Struggles in a Belfast Community. 250 pp.*

Crook, I. and **D.** Revolution in a Chinese Village. *Ten Mile Inn. 216 pp., illustrated.*

Etzioni-Halevy, E. Political Manipulation and Administrative Power. *A Comparative Study. About 200 pp.*

Fielding, N. The National Front. *About 250 pp.*

● **Hechter, Michael.** Internal Colonialism. *The Celtic Fringe in British National Development, 1536–1966. 380 pp.*

Kornhauser, William. The Politics of Mass Society. *272 pp. 20 tables.*

Korpi, W. The Working Class in Welfare Capitalism. *Work, Unions and Politics in Sweden. 472 pp.*

Kroes, R. Soldiers and Students. *A Study of Right- and Left-wing Students. 174 pp.*

Martin, Roderick. Sociology of Power. *About 272 pp.*

Merquior, J. G. Rousseau and Weber. *A Study in the Theory of Legitimacy. About 288 pp.*

Myrdal, Gunnar. The Political Element in the Development of Economic Theory. *Translated from the German by Paul Streeten. 282 pp.*

Varma, B. N. The Sociology and Politics of Development. *A Theoretical Study. 236 pp.*

Wong, S.-L. Sociology and Socialism in Contemporary China. *160 pp.*

Wootton, Graham. Workers, Unions and the State. *188 pp.*

CRIMINOLOGY

Ancel, Marc. Social Defence: *A Modern Approach to Criminal Problems. Foreword by Leon Radzinowicz. 240 pp.*

Athens, L. Violent Criminal Acts and Actors. *104 pp.*

Cain, Maureen E. Society and the Policeman's Role. *326 pp.*

Cloward, Richard A. and **Ohlin, Lloyd E.** Delinquency and Opportunity: *A Theory of Delinquent Gangs. 248 pp.*

Downes, David M. The Delinquent Solution. *A Study in Subcultural Theory. 296 pp.*

Friedlander, Kate. The Psycho-Analytical Approach to Juvenile Delinquency: *Theory, Case Studies, Treatment. 320 pp.*

Gleuck, Sheldon and **Eleanor.** Family Environment and Delinquency. *With the statistical assistance of Rose W. Kneznek. 340 pp.*

Lopez-Rey, Manuel. Crime. *An Analytical Appraisal. 288 pp.*

Mannheim, Hermann. Comparative Criminology: *A Text Book. Two volumes. 442 pp. and 380 pp.*

Morris, Terence. The Criminal Area: *A Study in Social Ecology. Foreword by Hermann Mannheim. 232 pp. 25 tables. 4 maps.*

Rock, Paul. Making People Pay. *338 pp.*

● **Taylor, Ian, Walton, Paul** and **Young, Jock.** The New Criminology. *For a Social Theory of Deviance. 325 pp.*

● **Taylor, Ian, Walton, Paul** and **Young, Jock.** (Eds) Critical Criminology. *268 pp.*

SOCIAL PSYCHOLOGY

Bagley, Christopher. The Social Psychology of the Epileptic Child. *320 pp.*

Brittan, Arthur. Meanings and Situations. *224 pp.*

Carroll, J. Break-Out from the Crystal Palace. *200 pp.*

● **Fleming, C. M.** Adolescence: Its Social Psychology. *With an Introduction to recent findings from the fields of Anthropology, Physiology, Medicine, Psychometrics and Sociometry. 288 pp.*

● The Social Psychology of Education: *An Introduction and Guide to Its Study. 136 pp.*

Linton, Ralph. The Cultural Background of Personality. *132 pp.*

● **Mayo, Elton.** The Social Problems of an Industrial Civilization. *With an Appendix on the Political Problem. 180 pp.*

Ottaway, A. K. C. Learning Through Group Experience. *176 pp.*

Plummer, Ken. Sexual Stigma. *An Interactionist Account. 254 pp.*

● **Rose, Arnold M.** (Ed.) Human Behaviour and Social Processes: *an Interactionist Approach. Contributions by Arnold M. Rose, Ralph H. Turner, Anselm Strauss, Everett C. Hughes, E. Franklin Frazier, Howard S. Becker et al. 696 pp.*

Smelser, Neil J. Theory of Collective Behaviour. *448 pp.*

Stephenson, Geoffrey M. The Development of Conscience. *128 pp.*

Young, Kimball. Handbook of Social Psychology. *658 pp. 16 figures. 10 tables.*

SOCIOLOGY OF THE FAMILY

Bell, Colin R. Middle Class Families: *Social and Geographical Mobility. 224 pp.*
Burton, Lindy. Vulnerable Children. *272 pp.*
Gavron, Hannah. The Captive Wife: *Conflicts of Household Mothers. 190 pp.*
George, Victor and **Wilding, Paul.** Motherless Families. *248 pp.*
Klein, Josephine. Samples from English Cultures.
   1. Three Preliminary Studies and Aspects of Adult Life in England. *447 pp.*
   2. Child-Rearing Practices and Index. *247 pp.*
Klein, Viola. The Feminine Character. *History of an Ideology. 244 pp.*
McWhinnie, Alexina M. Adopted Children. *How They Grow Up. 304 pp.*
● **Morgan, D. H. J.** Social Theory and the Family. *About 320 pp.*
● **Myrdal, Alva** and **Klein, Viola.** Women's Two Roles: *Home and Work. 238 pp.*
   27 tables.
Parsons, Talcott and **Bales, Robert F.** Family: Socialization and Interaction Process. *In collaboration with James Olds, Morris Zelditch and Philip E. Slater. 456 pp. 50 figures and tables.*

SOCIAL SERVICES

Bastide, Roger. The Sociology of Mental Disorder. *Translated from the French by Jean McNeil. 260 pp.*
Carlebach, Julius. Caring For Children in Trouble. *266 pp.*
George, Victor. Foster Care. *Theory and Practice. 234 pp.*
   Social Security: *Beveridge and After. 258 pp.*
George, V. and **Wilding, P.** Motherless Families. *248 pp.*
● **Goetschius, George W.** Working with Community Groups. *256 pp.*
Goetschius, George W. and **Tash, Joan.** Working with Unattached Youth. *416 pp.*
Heywood, Jean S. Children in Care. *The Development of the Service for the Deprived Child. Third revised edition. 284 pp.*
King, Roy D., Ranes, Norma V. and **Tizard, Jack.** Patterns of Residential Care. *356 pp.*
Leigh, John. Young People and Leisure. *256 pp.*
● **Mays, John.** (Ed.) Penelope Hall's Social Services of England and Wales. *368 pp.*
Morris, Mary. Voluntary Work and the Welfare State. *300 pp.*
Nokes, P. L. The Professional Task in Welfare Practice. *152 pp.*
Timms, Noel. Psychiatric Social Work in Great Britain (1939–1962). *280 pp.*
●   Social Casework: *Principles and Practice. 256 pp.*

SOCIOLOGY OF EDUCATION

Banks, Olive. Parity and Prestige in English Secondary Education: a Study in Educational Sociology. *272 pp.*
● **Blyth, W. A. L.** English Primary Education. *A Sociological Description.*
   2. Background. *168 pp.*
Collier, K. G. The Social Purposes of Education: *Personal and Social Values in Education. 268 pp.*
Evans, K. M. Sociometry and Education. *158 pp.*
● **Ford, Julienne.** Social Class and the Comprehensive School. *192 pp.*
Foster, P. J. Education and Social Change in Ghana. *336 pp. 3 maps.*
Fraser, W. R. Education and Society in Modern France. *150 pp.*
Grace, Gerald R. Role Conflict and the Teacher. *150 pp.*
Hans, Nicholas. New Trends in Education in the Eighteenth Century. *278 pp. 19 tables.*
●   Comparative Education: *A Study of Educational Factors and Traditions. 360 pp.*
● **Hargreaves, David.** Interpersonal Relations and Education. *432 pp.*
●   Social Relations in a Secondary School. *240 pp.*
   School Organization and Pupil Involvement. *A Study of Secondary Schools.*

- **Mannheim, Karl** and **Stewart, W. A. C.** An Introduction to the Sociology of Education. *206 pp.*
- **Musgrove, F.** Youth and the Social Order. *176 pp.*
- **Ottaway, A. K. C.** Education and Society: An Introduction to the Sociology of Education. *With an Introduction by W. O. Lester Smith. 212 pp.*

Peers, Robert. Adult Education: *A Comparative Study. Revised edition. 398 pp.*

Stratta, Erica. The Education of Borstal Boys. *A Study of their Educational Experiences prior to, and during, Borstal Training. 256 pp.*

- **Taylor, P. H., Reid, W. A.** and **Holley, B. J.** The English Sixth Form. *A Case Study in Curriculum Research. 198 pp.*

SOCIOLOGY OF CULTURE

Eppel, E. M. and **M.** Adolescents and Morality: *A Study of some Moral Values and Dilemmas of Working Adolescents in the Context of a changing Climate of Opinion. Foreword by W. J. H. Sprott. 268 pp. 39 tables.*

- **Fromm, Erich.** The Fear of Freedom. *286 pp.*
- The Sane Society. *400 pp.*

Johnson, L. The Cultural Critics. *From Matthew Arnold to Raymond Williams. 233 pp.*

Mannheim, Karl. Essays on the Sociology of Culture. *Edited by Ernst Mannheim in co-operation with Paul Kecskemeti. Editorial Note by Adolph Lowe. 280 pp.*

Merquior, J. G. The Veil and the Mask. *Essays on Culture and Ideology. Foreword by Ernest Gellner. 140 pp.*

Zijderfeld, A. C. On Clichés. *The Supersedure of Meaning by Function in Modernity. 150 pp.*

SOCIOLOGY OF RELIGION

Argyle, Michael and **Beit-Hallahmi, Benjamin.** The Social Psychology of Religion. *256 pp.*

Glasner, Peter E. The Sociology of Secularisation. *A Critique of a Concept. 146 pp.*

Hall, J. R. The Ways Out. *Utopian Communal Groups in an Age of Babylon. 280 pp.*

Ranson, S., Hinings, B. and **Bryman, A.** Clergy, Ministers and Priests. *216 pp.*

Stark, Werner. The Sociology of Religion. *A Study of Christendom.*

Volume II. *Sectarian Religion. 368 pp.*

Volume III. *The Universal Church. 464 pp.*

Volume IV. *Types of Religious Man. 352 pp.*

Volume V. *Types of Religious Culture. 464 pp.*

Turner, B. S. Weber and Islam. *216 pp.*

Watt, W. Montgomery. Islam and the Integration of Society. *320 pp.*

SOCIOLOGY OF ART AND LITERATURE

Jarvie, Ian C. Towards a Sociology of the Cinema. *A Comparative Essay on the Structure and Functioning of a Major Entertainment Industry. 405 pp.*

Rust, Frances S. Dance in Society. *An Analysis of the Relationships between the Social Dance and Society in England from the Middle Ages to the Present Day. 256 pp. 8 pp. of plates.*

Schücking, L. L. The Sociology of Literary Taste. *112 pp.*

Wolff, Janet. Hermeneutic Philosophy and the Sociology of Art. *150 pp.*

SOCIOLOGY OF KNOWLEDGE

Diesing, P. Patterns of Discovery in the Social Sciences. *262 pp.*

● **Douglas, J. D.** (Ed.) Understanding Everyday Life. *370 pp.*
● **Hamilton, P.** Knowledge and Social Structure. *174 pp.*
  Jarvie, I. C. Concepts and Society. *232 pp.*
  Mannheim, Karl. Essays on the Sociology of Knowledge. *Edited by Paul Kecskemeti. Editorial Note by Adolph Lowe. 353 pp.*
  Remmling, Gunter W. The Sociology of Karl Mannheim. *With a Bibliographical Guide to the Sociology of Knowledge, Ideological Analysis, and Social Planning. 255 pp.*
  Remmling, Gunter W. (Ed.) Towards the Sociology of Knowledge. *Origin and Development of a Sociological Thought Style. 463 pp.*
  Scheler, M. Problems of a Sociology of Knowledge. *Trans. by M. S. Frings. Edited and with an Introduction by K. Stikkers. 232 pp.*

URBAN SOCIOLOGY

  Aldridge, M. The British New Towns. *A Programme Without a Policy. 232 pp.*
  Ashworth, William. The Genesis of Modern British Town Planning: *A Study in Economic and Social History of the Nineteenth and Twentieth Centuries. 288 pp.*
  Brittan, A. The Privatised World. *196 pp.*
  Cullingworth, J. B. Housing Needs and Planning Policy: *A Restatement of the Problems of Housing Need and 'Overspill' in England and Wales. 232 pp. 44 tables. 8 maps.*
  Dickinson, Robert E. City and Region: *A Geographical Interpretation. 608 pp. 125 figures.*
    The West European City: *A Geographical Interpretation. 600 pp. 129 maps. 29 plates.*
  Humphreys, Alexander J. New Dubliners: *Urbanization and the Irish Family. Foreword by George C. Homans. 304 pp.*
  Jackson, Brian. Working Class Community: *Some General Notions raised by a Series of Studies in Northern England. 192 pp.*
● **Mann, P. H.** An Approach to Urban Sociology. *240 pp.*
  Mellor, J. R. Urban Sociology in an Urbanized Society. *326 pp.*
  Morris, R. N. and **Mogey, J.** The Sociology of Housing. *Studies at Berinsfield. 232 pp. 4 pp. plates.*
  Mullan, R. Stevenage Ltd. *About 250 pp.*
  Rex, J. and **Tomlinson, S.** Colonial Immigrants in a British City. *A Class Analysis. 368 pp.*
  Rosser, C. and **Harris, C.** The Family and Social Change. *A Study of Family and Kinship in a South Wales Town. 352 pp. 8 maps.*
● **Stacey, Margaret, Batsone, Eric, Bell, Colin** and **Thurcott, Anne.** Power, Persistence and Change. *A Second Study of Banbury. 196 pp.*

RURAL SOCIOLOGY

  Mayer, Adrian C. Peasants in the Pacific. *A Study of Fiji Indian Rural Society. 248 pp. 20 plates.*
  Williams, W. M. The Sociology of an English Village: *Gosforth. 272 pp. 12 figures. 13 tables.*

SOCIOLOGY OF INDUSTRY AND DISTRIBUTION

  Dunkerley, David. The Foreman. *Aspects of Task and Structure. 192 pp.*
  Eldridge, J. E. T. Industrial Disputes. *Essays in the Sociology of Industrial Relations. 288 pp.*
  Hollowell, Peter G. The Lorry Driver. *272 pp.*
● **Oxaal, I., Barnett, T.** and **Booth, D.** (Eds) Beyond the Sociology of Development.

8

Economy and Society in Latin America and Africa. 295 pp.

Smelser, Neil J. Social Change in the Industrial Revolution: *An Application of Theory to the Lancashire Cotton Industry, 1770–1840. 468 pp. 12 figures. 14 tables.*

Watson, T. J. The Personnel Managers. *A Study in the Sociology of Work and Employment, 262 pp.*

ANTHROPOLOGY

Brandel-Syrier, Mia. Reeftown Elite. *A Study of Social Mobility in a Modern African Community on the Reef. 376 pp.*

Dickie-Clark, H. F. The Marginal Situation. *A Sociological Study of a Coloured Group. 236 pp.*

Dube, S. C. Indian Village. *Foreword by Morris Edward Opler. 276 pp. 4 plates.*
India's Changing Villages: *Human Factors in Community Development. 260 pp. 8 plates. 1 map.*

Fei, H.-T. Peasant Life in China. *A Field Study of Country Life in the Yangtze Valley. With a foreword by Bronislaw Malinowski. 328 pp. 16 pp. plates.*

Firth, Raymond. Malay Fishermen. *Their Peasant Economy. 420 pp. 17 pp. plates.*

Gulliver, P. H. Social Control in an African Society: a Study of the Arusha, Agricultural Masai of Northern Tanganyika. *320 pp. 8 plates. 10 figures.*
Family Herds. *288 pp.*

Jarvie, Ian C. The Revolution in Anthropology. *268 pp.*

Little, Kenneth L. Mende of Sierra Leone. *308 pp. and folder.*
Negroes in Britain. *With a New Introduction and Contemporary Study by Leonard Bloom. 320 pp.*

Tambs-Lyche, H. London Patidars. *About 180 pp.*

Madan, G. R. Western Sociologists on Indian Society. *Marx, Spencer, Weber, Durkheim, Pareto. 384 pp.*

Mayer, A. C. Peasants in the Pacific. *A Study of Fiji Indian Rural Society. 248 pp.*

Meer, Fatima. Race and Suicide in South Africa. *325 pp.*

Smith, Raymond T. The Negro Family in British Guiana: *Family Structure and Social Status in the Villages. With a Foreword by Meyer Fortes. 314 pp. 8 plates. 1 figure. 4 maps.*

SOCIOLOGY AND PHILOSOPHY

Adriaansens, H. Talcott Parsons and the Conceptual Dilemma. *About 224 pp.*

Barnsley, John H. The Social Reality of Ethics. *A Comparative Analysis of Moral Codes. 448 pp.*

Diesing, Paul. Patterns of Discovery in the Social Sciences. *362 pp.*

● **Douglas, Jack D.** (Ed.) Understanding Everyday Life. *Toward the Reconstruction of Sociological Knowledge. Contributions by Alan F. Blum, Aaron W. Cicourel, Norman K. Denzin, Jack D. Douglas, John Heeren, Peter McHugh, Peter K. Manning, Melvin Power, Matthew Speier, Roy Turner, D. Lawrence Wieder, Thomas P. Wilson and Don H. Zimmerman. 370 pp.*

Gorman, Robert A. The Dual Vision. *Alfred Schutz and the Myth of Phenomenological Social Science. 240 pp.*

Jarvie, Ian C. Concepts and Society. *216 pp.*

Kilminster, R. Praxis and Method. *A Sociological Dialogue with Lukács, Gramsci and the Early Frankfurt School. 334 pp.*

● **Pelz, Werner.** The Scope of Understanding in Sociology. *Towards a More Radical Reorientation in the Social Humanistic Sciences. 283 pp.*

Roche, Maurice. Phenomenology, Language and the Social Sciences. *371 pp.*

Sahay, Arun. Sociological Analysis. *212 pp.*

● **Slater, P.** Origin and Significance of the Frankfurt School. *A Marxist Perspective. 185 pp.*

Spurling, L. Phenomenology and the Social World. *The Philosophy of Merleau-Ponty and its Relation to the Social Sciences. 222 pp.*

Wilson, H. T. The American Ideology. *Science, Technology and Organization as Modes of Rationality. 368 pp.*

International Library of Anthropology
General Editor Adam Kuper

● **Ahmed, A. S.** Millennium and Charisma Among Pathans. *A Critical Essay in Social Anthropology. 192 pp.*
Pukhtun Economy and Society. *Traditional Structure and Economic Development. About 360 pp.*

Barth, F. Selected Essays. *Volume I. About 250 pp.* Selected Essays. *Volume II. About 250 pp.*

Brown, Paula. The Chimbu. *A Study of Change in the New Guinea Highlands. 151 pp.*

Foner, N. Jamaica Farewell. *200 pp.*

Gudeman, Stephen. Relationships, Residence and the Individual. *A Rural Panamanian Community. 288 pp. 11 plates, 5 figures, 2 maps, 10 tables.*
The Demise of a Rural Economy. *From Subsistence to Capitalism in a Latin American Village. 160 pp.*

Hamnett, Ian. Chieftainship and Legitimacy. *An Anthropological Study of Executive Law in Lesotho. 163 pp.*

Hanson, F. Allan. Meaning in Culture. *127 pp.*

Hazan, H. The Limbo People. *A Study of the Constitution of the Time Universe Among the Aged. About 192 pp.*

Humphreys, S. C. Anthropology and the Greeks. *288 pp.*

Karp, I. Fields of Change Among the Iteso of Kenya. *140 pp.*

Lloyd, P. C. Power and Independence. *Urban Africans' Perception of Social Inequality. 264 pp.*

Parry, J. P. Caste and Kinship in Kangra. *352 pp. Illustrated.*

Pettigrew, Joyce. Robber Noblemen. *A Study of the Political System of the Sikh Jats. 284 pp.*

Street, Brian V. The Savage in Literature. *Representations of 'Primitive' Society in English Fiction, 1858–1920. 207 pp.*

Van Den Berghe, Pierre L. Power and Privilege at an African University. *278 pp.*

International Library of Phenomenology and Moral Sciences
General Editor John O'Neill

Apel, K.-O. Towards a Transformation of Philosophy. *308 pp.*

Bologh, R. W. Dialectical Phenomenology. *Marx's Method. 287 pp.*

Fekete, J. The Critical Twilight. *Explorations in the Ideology of Anglo-American Literary Theory from Eliot to McLuhan. 300 pp.*

Medina, A. Reflection, Time and the Novel. *Towards a Communicative Theory of Literature. 143 pp.*

International Library of Social Policy
General Editor Kathleen Jones

Bayley, M. Mental Handicap and Community Care. *426 pp.*

Bottoms, A. E. and **McClean, J. D.** Defendants in the Criminal Process. *284 pp.*

Bradshaw, J. The Family Fund. *An Initiative in Social Policy. About 224 pp.*

Butler, J. R. Family Doctors and Public Policy. *208 pp.*
Davies, Martin. Prisoners of Society. *Attitudes and Aftercare. 204 pp.*
Gittus, Elizabeth. Flats, Families and the Under-Fives. *285 pp.*
Holman, Robert. Trading in Children. *A Study of Private Fostering. 355 pp.*
Jeffs, A. Young People and the Youth Service. *160 pp.*
Jones, Howard and Cornes, Paul. Open Prisons. *288 pp.*
Jones, Kathleen. History of the Mental Health Service. *428 pp.*
Jones, Kathleen with **Brown, John, Cunningham, W. J., Roberts, Julian** and
    Williams, Peter. Opening the Door. *A Study of New Policies for the Mentally*
    Handicapped. 278 pp.
Karn, Valerie. Retiring to the Seaside. *400 pp. 2 maps. Numerous tables.*
King, R. D. and **Elliot, K. W.** Albany: Birth of a Prison—End of an Era. *394 pp.*
Thomas, J. E. The English Prison Officer since 1850: *A Study in Conflict. 258 pp.*
Walton, R. G. Women in Social Work. *303 pp.*
● **Woodward, J.** To Do the Sick No Harm. *A Study of the British Voluntary Hospital*
    System to 1875. 234 pp.

International Library of Welfare and Philosophy
General Editors   Noel Timms and David Watson

● **McDermott, F. E.** (Ed.) Self-Determination in Social Work. *A Collection of Essays*
    on Self-determination and Related Concepts by Philosophers and Social Work
    Theorists. Contributors: F. P. Biestek, S. Bernstein, A. Keith-Lucas, D. Sayer,
    H. H. Perelman, C. Whittington, R. F. Stalley, F. E. McDermott, I. Berlin, H. J.
    McCloskey, H. L. A. Hart, J. Wilson, A. I. Melden, S. I. Benn. 254 pp.
● **Plant, Raymond.** Community and Ideology. *104 pp.*
   Ragg, Nicholas M. People Not Cases. *A Philosophical Approach to Social Work.*
    168 pp.
● **Timms, Noel** and **Watson, David.** (Eds) Talking About Welfare. *Readings in*
    Philosophy and Social Policy. Contributors: T. H. Marshall, R. B. Brandt, G. H.
    von Wright, K. Nielsen, M. Cranston, R. M. Titmuss, R. S. Downie, E. Telfer, D.
    Donnison, J. Benson, P. Leonard, A. Keith-Lucas, D. Walsh, I. T. Ramsey.
    320 pp.
● Philosophy in Social Work. *250 pp.*
● **Weale, A.** Equality and Social Policy. *164 pp.*

Library of Social Work
General Editor   Noel Timms

● **Baldock, Peter.** Community Work and Social Work. *140 pp.*
○ **Beedell, Christopher.** Residential Life with Children. *210 pp. Crown 8vo.*
● **Berry, Juliet.** Daily Experience in Residential Life. *A Study of Children and their*
    Care-givers. 202 pp.
○ Social Work with Children. *190 pp. Crown 8vo.*
● **Brearley, C. Paul.** Residential Work with the Elderly. *116 pp.*
● Social Work, Ageing and Society. *126 pp.*
● **Cheetham, Juliet.** Social Work with Immigrants. *240 pp. Crown 8vo.*
● **Cross, Crispin P.** (Ed.) Interviewing and Communication in Social Work.
    Contributions by C. P. Cross, D. Laurenson, B. Strutt, S. Raven. 192 pp. Crown
    8vo.

- **Curnock, Kathleen** and **Hardiker, Pauline.** Towards Practice Theory. *Skills and Methods in Social Assessments. 208 pp.*
- **Davies, Bernard.** The Use of Groups in Social Work Practice. *158 pp.*
- **Davies, Martin.** Support Systems in Social Work. *144 pp.*
  Ellis, June. (Ed.) West African Families in Britain. *A Meeting of Two Cultures.* Contributions by Pat Stapleton, Vivien Biggs. *150 pp. 1 Map.*
- **Hart, John.** Social Work and Sexual Conduct. *230 pp.*
- **Hutten, Joan M.** Short-Term Contracts in Social Work. *Contributions by Stella M. Hall, Elsie Osborne, Mannie Sher, Eva Sternberg, Elizabeth Tuters. 134 pp.*
  Jackson, Michael P. and **Valencia, B. Michael.** Financial Aid Through Social Work. *140 pp.*
- **Jones, Howard.** The Residential Community. *A Setting for Social Work. 150 pp.*
- (Ed.) Towards a New Social Work. *Contributions by Howard Jones, D. A. Fowler, J. R. Cypher, R. G. Walton, Geoffrey Mungham, Philip Priestley, Ian Shaw, M. Bartley, R. Deacon, Irwin Epstein, Geoffrey Pearson. 184 pp.*
  Jones, Ray and **Pritchard, Colin.** (Eds) Social Work With Adolescents. *Contributions by Ray Jones, Colin Pritchard, Jack Dunham, Florence Rossetti, Andrew Kerslake, John Burns, William Gregory, Graham Templeman, Kenneth E. Reid, Audrey Taylor. About 170 pp.*
- ○ **Jordon, William.** The Social Worker in Family Situations. *160 pp. Crown 8vo.*
- **Laycock, A. L.** Adolescents and Social Work. *128 pp. Crown 8vo.*
- **Lees, Ray.** Politics and Social Work. *128 pp. Crown 8vo.*
- Research Strategies for Social Welfare. *112 pp. Tables.*
- ○ **McCullough, M. K.** and **Ely, Peter J.** Social Work with Groups. *127 pp. Crown 8vo.*
- **Moffett, Jonathan.** Concepts in Casework Treatment. *128 pp. Crown 8vo.*
  Parsloe, Phyllida. Juvenile Justice in Britain and the United States. *The Balance of Needs and Rights. 336 pp.*
- **Plant, Raymond.** Social and Moral Theory in Casework. *112 pp. Crown 8vo.*
  Priestley, Philip, Fears, Denise and **Fuller, Roger.** Justice for Juveniles. *The 1969 Children and Young Persons Act: A Case for Reform? 128 pp.*
- **Pritchard, Colin** and **Taylor, Richard.** Social Work: Reform or Revolution? *170 pp.*
- ○ **Pugh, Elisabeth.** Social Work in Child Care. *128 pp. Crown 8vo.*
- **Robinson, Margaret.** Schools and Social Work. *282 pp.*
- ○ **Ruddock, Ralph.** Roles and Relationships. *128 pp. Crown 8vo.*
- **Sainsbury, Eric.** Social Diagnosis in Casework. *118 pp. Crown 8vo.*
- Social Work with Families. *Perceptions of Social Casework among Clients of a Family Service. 188 pp.*
  Seed, Philip. The Expansion of Social Work in Britain. *128 pp. Crown 8vo.*
- **Shaw, John.** The Self in Social Work. *124 pp.*
  Smale, Gerald G. Prophecy, Behaviour and Change. *An Examination of Self-fulfilling Prophecies in Helping Relationships. 116 pp. Crown 8vo.*
  Smith, Gilbert. Social Need. *Policy, Practice and Research. 155 pp.*
- Social Work and the Sociology of Organisations. *124 pp. Revised edition.*
- **Sutton, Carole.** Psychology for Social Workers and Counsellors. *An Introduction. 248 pp.*
- **Timms, Noel.** Language of Social Casework. *122 pp. Crown 8vo.*
- Recording in Social Work. *124 pp. Crown 8vo.*
- **Todd, F. Joan.** Social Work with the Mentally Subnormal. *96 pp. Crown 8vo.*
- **Walrond-Skinner, Sue.** Family Therapy. *The Treatment of Natural Systems. 172 pp.*
- **Warham, Joyce.** An Introduction to Administration for Social Workers. *Revised edition. 112 pp.*
- An Open Case. *The Organisational Context of Social Work. 172 pp.*
- ○ **Wittenberg, Isca Salzberger.** Psycho-Analytic Insight and Relationships. *A Kleinian Approach. 196 pp. Crown 8vo.*

Primary Socialization, Language and Education
General Editor   Basil Bernstein

Adlam, Diana S., *with the assistance of Geoffrey Turner and Lesley Lineker.* Code in Context. *272 pp.*

Bernstein, Basil. Class, Codes and Control. *3 volumes.*
- 1. *Theoretical Studies Towards a Sociology of Language. 254 pp.*
  2. *Applied Studies Towards a Sociology of Language. 377 pp.*
- 3. *Towards a Theory of Educational Transmission. 167 pp.*

Brandis, W. and **Bernstein, B.** Selection and Control. *176 pp.*

Brandis, Walter and **Henderson, Dorothy.** Social Class, Language and Communication. *288 pp.*

Cook-Gumperz, Jenny. Social Control and Socialization. *A Study of Class Differences in the Language of Maternal Control. 290 pp.*

- **Gahagan, D. M.** and **G. A.** Talk Reform. *Exploration in Language for Infant School Children. 160 pp.*

Hawkins, P. R. Social Class, the Nominal Group and Verbal Strategies. *About 220 pp.*

Robinson, W. P. and **Rackstraw, Susan D. A.** A Question of Answers. *2 volumes. 192 pp. and 180 pp.*

Turner, Geoffrey J. and **Mohan, Bernard A.** A Linguistic Description and Computer Programme for Children's Speech. *208 pp.*

Reports of the Institute of Community Studies

Baker, J. The Neighbourhood Advice Centre. A Community Project in Camden. *320 pp.*

- **Cartwright, Ann.** Patients and their Doctors. *A Study of General Practice. 304 pp.*

Dench, Geoff. Maltese in London. *A Case-study in the Erosion of Ethnic Consciousness. 302 pp.*

Jackson, Brian and **Marsden, Dennis.** Education and the Working Class: *Some General Themes Raised by a Study of 88 Working-class Children in a Northern Industrial City. 268 pp. 2 folders.*

Marris, Peter. The Experience of Higher Education. *232 pp. 27 tables.*

- Loss and Change. *192 pp.*

Marris, Peter and **Rein, Martin.** Dilemmas of Social Reform. *Poverty and Community Action in the United States. 256 pp.*

Marris, Peter and **Somerset, Anthony.** African Businessmen. *A Study of Entrepreneurship and Development in Kenya. 256 pp.*

Mills, Richard. Young Outsiders: *a Study in Alternative Communities. 216 pp.*

Runciman, W. G. Relative Deprivation and Social Justice. *A Study of Attitudes to Social Inequality in Twentieth-Century England. 352 pp.*

Willmott, Peter. Adolescent Boys in East London. *230 pp.*

Willmott, Peter and **Young, Michael.** Family and Class in a London Suburb. *202 pp. 47 tables.*

Young, Michael and **McGeeney, Patrick.** Learning Begins at Home. *A Study of a Junior School and its Parents. 128 pp.*

Young, Michael and **Willmott, Peter.** Family and Kinship in East London. *Foreword by Richard M. Titmuss. 252 pp. 39 tables.*

The Symmetrical Family. *410 pp.*

Reports of the Institute for Social Studies in Medical Care

Cartwright, Ann, Hockey, Lisbeth and **Anderson, John J.** Life Before Death. *310 pp.*
Dunnell, Karen and **Cartwright, Ann.** Medicine Takers, Prescribers and Hoarders. *190 pp.*
Farrell, C. My Mother Said. . . *A Study of the Way Young People Learned About Sex and Birth Control. 288 pp.*

Medicine, Illness and Society
General Editor W. M. Williams

Hall, David J. Social Relations & Innovation. *Changing the State of Play in Hospitals. 232 pp.*
Hall, David J. and **Stacey, M.** (Eds) Beyond Separation. *234 pp.*
Robinson, David. The Process of Becoming Ill. *142 pp.*
Stacey, Margaret *et al.* Hospitals, Children and Their Families. *The Report of a Pilot Study. 202 pp.*
Stimson, G. V. and **Webb, B.** Going to See the Doctor. *The Consultation Process in General Practice. 155 pp.*

Monographs in Social Theory
General Editor Arthur Brittan

● **Barnes, B.** Scientific Knowledge and Sociological Theory. *192 pp.*
Bauman, Zygmunt. Culture as Praxis. *204 pp.*
● **Dixon, Keith.** Sociological Theory. *Pretence and Possibility. 142 pp.*
The Sociology of Belief. *Fallacy and Foundation. About 160 pp.*
Goff, T. W. Marx and Mead. *Contributions to a Sociology of Knowledge. 176 pp.*
Meltzer, B. N., Petras, J. W. and **Reynolds, L. T.** Symbolic Interactionism. *Genesis, Varieties and Criticisms. 144 pp.*
● **Smith, Anthony D.** The Concept of Social Change. *A Critique of the Functionalist Theory of Social Change. 208 pp.*

Routledge Social Science Journals

The British Journal of Sociology. *Editor – Angus Stewart; Associate Editor – Leslie Sklair. Vol. 1, No. 1 – March 1950 and Quarterly. Roy. 8vo. All back issues available. An international journal publishing original papers in the field of sociology and related areas.*
Community Work. *Edited by David Jones and Marjorie Mayo. 1973. Published annually.*
Economy and Society. *Vol. 1, No. 1. February 1972 and Quarterly. Metric Roy. 8vo. A journal for all social scientists covering sociology, philosophy, anthropology, economics and history. All back numbers available.*

Ethnic and Racial Studies. *Editor – John Stone. Vol. 1 – 1978. Published quarterly.*

Religion. Journal of Religion and Religions. *Chairman of Editorial Board, Ninian Smart. Vol. 1, No. 1, Spring 1971. A journal with an inter-disciplinary approach to the study of the phenomena of religion. All back numbers available.*

Sociology of Health and Illness. *A Journal of Medical Sociology. Editor – Alan Davies; Associate Editor – Ray Jobling. Vol. 1, Spring 1979. Published 3 times per annum.*

Year Book of Social Policy in Britain. *Edited by Kathleen Jones. 1971. Published annually.*

Social and Psychological Aspects of Medical Practice
Editor   Trevor Silverstone

Lader, Malcolm. Psychophysiology of Mental Illness. *280 pp.*

● **Silverstone, Trevor** and **Turner, Paul.** Drug Treatment in Psychiatry. *Revised edition. 256 pp.*

Whiteley, J. S. and **Gordon, J.** Group Approaches in Psychiatry. *240 pp.*